combination of

and visual

appropriated and

contemporary

the world,

to expressive

architecture.

Regionalism
the particulars o
It mines
and perceptions
about a truly

The work of these four architects shows that investigation of the local is a fundamental step in the rehumanization of architecture.

Concrete's
structural strength
variety is
explored by
architects aroun
giving rise
regiona

addresses
place and culture.
everyday life
for intimations
progressive future.

After a long

a building

concrete came

in the early

century

of realizing

new

history as
material,
to prominence
part of this
as a means
dynamic
forms.

In the twentieth

with its emphasis on

movements,

the truest and most

has regional roots

century,

international

much of

seminal invention

Concrete Regionalism

Catherine Slessor

With 258 illustrations, 104 in color

Thames & Hudson

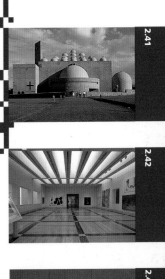

2.00 Traditional pueblo dwellings
Vernacular architecture embodies
a direct expression of the relationship
humankind has with landscape and
culture. Such immemorial sources
present the possibility of reinventing
architecture in the service of society.

Introduction
Rehumanizing Architecture

In an age of increased cultural and social homogenization, the issue of regionalism has assumed a renewed and timely importance. The history of the twentieth century has been dominated by rapacious globalization, the systematic erosion of difference and plurality and the commodification of culture. While representing material advancement and social liberalization, these universalizing forces invariably involve the destruction of traditional cultures and a disengagement with the past. What is now most prized by the multinational corporations stalking the globe is a universal, undifferentiated abacus upon which the ebb and flow of value-free exchange and profit can be facilitated. Such issues may appear remote from the immediate practice of architecture, but they have transformed the ground rules of large-scale building production. Architecture is in danger of becoming a marginalized freemasonry, its creative potential reduced to eclectic wrapping paper adorning slabs of dehumanized corporate space planning. From Dallas to Dacca, the outcome of this banal hegemony of the built environment is only too apparent.

Architecture's ambivalent relationship with modern capitalism and its growing dependence on fashionable treatises and self-justifying theories have resulted in the neglect of diverse physical environments that have the potential to deliver empirical inspiration for art and invention. Yet despite the richness of vernacular sources, the propensity to acknowledge the relevance of regionalism in the developed world has been slow in coming. In 1979 the American critic Arthur Drexler noted an important strain of regionally inspired modernism in the work of such architects as Alvar Aalto, Marcel Breuer and Richard Neutra. Since then, the idea of regional

2.00 Kauffman House
The iconic Kauffman House in Palm Springs was designed by Richard Neutra. A covered deck frames a commanding and contemplative view of distant mountains in the Japanese tradition of borrowed landscape (whereby a view is precisely and statically framed by the positioning of objects and plants), which is reinforced by a gnarled branch set on a low table.

sensitivity has been explored and encouraged through the writings of such historians and theorists as Christian Norberg-Schultz, Kenneth Frampton and William Curtis. As Curtis has observed, 'There is certainly a mood gathering which rejects the glib reproduction of international formulae and which seeks out continuities with local traditions. The moment is right for the assertion of an architectural value system that eschews the aridity of offhand utilitarianism and the bogus remedy of phoney historicism.'[1] Frampton's definition of what he calls 'critical regionalism' has established an important framework for discourse and debate: 'It is not intended to denote the vernacular as this was once spontaneously produced by the combined interaction of climate, culture, myth and craft, but rather to identify those recent regional "schools" whose primary aim is to reflect and serve the limited constituencies in which they are grounded.'[2]

Regionalism addresses the particulars of place and culture. It mines everyday life and perception for intimations about a truly progressive future. It aims to sustain a close and continuous relationship between architecture and the local community it serves. Crucially, it learns from experience. It tinkers, crafts, accepts, rejects, adjusts and reacts. It is immutably rooted in the tangible realities of its situation: the history, geography, human values, economy, traditions, technology and cultural life of place.

Beyond architecture, regionalism's influence can be perceived in other artistic disciplines. Jazz, for instance, that most fundamental and influential creation of twentieth-century music, originated as a regional expression. Embedded in the polyglot culture of New Orleans at the turn of the century, its invention is inconceivable outside the particular milieu of African and

European traditions from which it sprang. In painting, the development of modern art as a revolutionary phenomenon was given significant impetus by profound introspection of particular events and places. Artists as diverse as Paul Gauguin, Edvard Munch and Diego Rivera all drew on local culture as sources for their art. Even Pablo Picasso, the quintessential international painter, displayed a compulsive intensity with established subject matter as in *Guernica* (1937), a coruscating study of conflict set in his Spanish homeland.

Music and painting are portable, transient media. Architecture, the most physical of all the arts, has the capacity to draw potent inspiration from place and examples of this resonate through history. The shift from Roman to Byzantine architecture, for instance, reflected quite simply a shift of geography. In the fourth century, Constantine, the first Christian emperor, moved the capital of the Roman empire to Byzantium. This displacement from Rome to an old Greek trading colony on the Bosphorous incited a revolutionary approach to architecture. A sensitivity to the history and traditions of Asia Minor and the Near East, combined with an acknowledgment of the modern contribution of Roman culture, generated a genuinely new form of architectural, spatial and technological expression, for example, Hagia Sophia, the church built by Justinian between 532 and 562. Inspired by Byzantium, the new architecture spread across the empire, to Ravenna, Venice, Rome and Gaul, where it spawned a wide range of expressions; again, the momentum that sparked these innovations was regionally derived.

Set against such major historical conflations of cultures is the equally important notion that invention may also arise from renewed awareness of place. It is this sort of regional rediscovery that fermented the Renaissance in Italy during the fifteenth century. The dominance of northern European regimes and Gothic architecture had long stifled the economic and political

2.00 *Guernica*
Pablo Picasso's *Guernica* portrays the horrors of the Spanish Civil War and derives its intensity from the resonance of its subject matter.

power of native trecento Italy. In Florence, the population passionately resented this foreign influence and an anti-Gothic movement emerged, based on a mixture of Guelph, Roman and Humanist elements. Sculpture and architecture in particular espoused the renewal of classic Roman forms, as well as a reassertion of Italian Romanesque traditions. Filippo Brunelleschi, architect of two great Florentine churches San Lorenzo and Santo Spirito and the iconic dome of the city's cathedral, sought to capture the manner in which the ancients had built and to reinvest his region with the grandeur and power of its past. It is impossible to imagine this extraordinary reorientation happening anywhere else in Europe: it was essentially place-inspired.

Even in the twentieth century, with its emphasis on international movements, much of the truest and most seminal invention had regional roots. The great American modernist Frank Lloyd Wright, for example, drew inspiration from rural life of the American Midwest. With its dominant horizontality alluding to the infinite sweep of the surrounding prairies and its walls made from local stone combined with a traditional timber frame, his house at Taliesin North in Wisconsin (1931) is an extension of the geological and topographic forms of the region. This was honest, sincere and unaffected architecture that sprang from the pragmatic values of the

2.00 Hagia Sophia
By moving the capital of the Empire to Constantinople (Istanbul), Constantine brought together techniques from all over the Mediterranean world – Roman, Persian and Christian. Justinian's church of Hagia Sophia combines all these influences on a scale never attempted before.

2.00 Taliesin West
The primeval power of the desert landscape is reflected in Frank Lloyd Wright's rugged complex of buildings at Taliesin West. The key to Wright's architecture was his intuitive ability to discern elements – even in such relatively obscure places as Wisconsin and Arizona – that had been neglected or undervalued for generations and to reinvigorate them in a magical, modern synthesis.

Midwest. At Taliesin West in Arizona (1938), Wright was influenced by another kind of landscape. The power of the desert's flatness, ruggedness, textures and colours inform a remarkable cluster of structures. Stepped terraces, low stone walls and flat roofs recall pueblo construction, while other structures hover lightly above the desert like Indian tents. Clearly related to tradition, Taliesin West is also a radical statement of invention.

Wright's genius was grounded in the discovery of the potential in apparently unpromising contexts, a kind of architectural alchemy. This epitomizes a quality that Alvar Aalto described as 'the gift of seeing the beautiful in everything'.[3] Aalto, like Wright, often built in places that lacked strong or cohesive architectural heritage, yet felt compelled to draw on such qualities that did exist. In his earliest buildings, Aalto reinterpreted basic Finnish sources – rural vernacular and nineteenth-century neoclassicism – but went on to develop a more resonant regionalism that redefined his country's relationship with its landscape and culture. Aalto's Villa Mairea (1941) is exemplary; part Nordic turf-roofed hut, part vernacular log cabin, intimate and organic, it also reflects the spare functionalism of newly industrialized Finland. Craftsmanship and rationalism are held in exquisite equilibrium.

Aalto's synthesis of the particular and the universal crystallizes an important strand of modernism. The capacity to absorb and transform a variety of sources and civilizations has played a central role in the work of

2.00 Kimbell Art Museum
In the Kimbell Art Museum at Fort Worth, Louis Kahn succeeded in unifying the particular and the universal. Other great modernists, such as Alvar Aalto, Jørn Utzon and Le Corbusier also combined the international and the regional to bring a continuous source of new possibilities and enrichment to architecture.

major architects with seemingly larger agendas, such as Le Corbusier, Louis Kahn and Jørn Utzon. The interaction of international and regional, old and new, contributed to the symbolic richness of individual works and suggested new formal possibilities. With hindsight, the arid tendencies of modernism have not always been the liberating forces of advancement their apologists claimed. A critical re-examination that gained new momentum in the postwar years attempted to find the right balance between the progressive ideals of modernization and the vernacular forms of particular regions. This was the age of notable individual achievement for such architects as Luis Barragán in Mexico, Kenzo Tange in Japan, Oscar Niemeyer in Brazil and Sverre Fehn in Norway, each of whom explored the symbiosis of international influence and the interpretation of their particular culture and society. The best of these buildings seemed able to draw upon indigenous wisdom without resorting to pastiche, penetrating beyond the superficial features of regional style to explore a more resonant architecture rooted in immemorial responses to landscape and climate.

When regionalism emerged in a European context during the 1980s, it was often in a populist or kitsch imitation of the vernacular. But there were developments of a more demanding intellectual nature that addressed particular regional attributes. Mario Botta in the Ticino canton of Switzerland, for example, attempted to translate the elemental character of southern Alpine vernacular into an architecture of pure forms, yet his work also engaged with the universal aspirations of modernism. A sensitivity to context and climate ran through the work of many contemporary Barcelona-based architects, such as Carlos Ferrater and Torres and Lapeña,

2.00 Garea House
Oscar Niemeyer's fluid,
biomorphic architecture
responds to the sinuous
contours and plant forms of
the tropical Brazilian landscape.
His own house in Rio de Janeiro
is a hieroglyph of concave
and convex incisions in the
lush terrain.

extending a Catalan lineage that stretched back to Coderch and the intense, fantastical architecture of Antoni Gaudí. By the late twentieth century most authentic traditions were either extinct or precariously under threat. In any case, architects could not simply appropriate and reuse these languages without fatally devaluing them; but they could conceive of new kinds of architecture that resonated with a specific cultural or natural landscape.

The quartet of architects considered here reflects differing philosophical and geographical backgrounds, but all are bound, to varying degrees, by an explicit connection to place. Their architecture shares apparent formal and material similarities based on a language of walls and planes (generally made of concrete), of earthbound masses penetrated and animated by light. Yet within this communal language are four vigorous and distinct dialects.

Striving to unite the culture of Japan with universal ideals of modernism, Tadao Ando embodies an especially astute regional consciousness. Based in Osaka rather than Tokyo, Ando's built work and theoretical writings formulate perhaps more clearly than any other architect of his generation a set of precepts that fuse the ideals of contemporary architecture with indigenous sensibilities and customs. In his small courtyard houses, often set within a dense urban fabric, Ando employs concrete to stress the taut homogeneity of its surface rather than its weight. Mass is transformed into a means of reflecting light and dematerializing space. While the cardinal importance of light is stressed in the writings of Kahn and Le Corbusier, Ando sees the paradox of spatial limpidity emerging out of light as being peculiarly pertinent to the Japanese character. The sensuousness of his buildings transcends their clinical geometry and minimal materiality.

2.00 Round House
Mario Botta abstracted and transformed Ticino's Alpine vernacular into pure geometry. This proved to be one of the most thoughtful strands of regionally inspired architecture to emerge in Europe during the 1980s.

Ando has exerted considerable influence on both Japanese and European designers, among them Wiel Arets, a Dutch architect who is gaining a growing international reputation. Like Ando, Arets is deliberately positioned at some remove from the fashionable mainstream; in Arets's case in the provincial town of Heerlen in southern Netherlands. Arets's work is possibly the least place-bound of the quartet, but despite his tendencies towards theoretical abstraction and metaphor, his work reflects aspects of early Dutch modernism. Its tectonic clarity depends on the very precise handling of materials – raw concrete, glass blocks, brick – and the way in which light is introduced into space. In some ways it also represents the continuation of a reciprocal dialogue between Europe and Japan that has existed since the early days of modernism. Traditional Japanese architecture had a profound influence on European modernists, who saw the simplicity and spatial egalitarianism of Japanese structures as an alternative to highly decorated and compartmentalized Western buildings.

Working in the vast tracts of the American Southwest, Antoine Predock explores a dialogue with the region's powerfully surreal landscape and its complex cultural ancestry to create an architecture that reaches beyond both historicism and regionalism. Like that of Wright and Aalto, Predock's work takes its impetus from concerns of site and programme, but while his architecture remains consistently spare, planar and primal, it is also richly inflected by ideas and images from such different sources as folklore, cyberspace and cultural marginalia.

Finally, in Mexico, Ricardo Legorreta poetically embodies an elusive synthesis of local and global that encompasses the monumental abstraction of ancient Mesoamerican civilizations and the vibrancy of Hispanic colonization. Legorreta extends a basic language of bold volumes, courtyard forms, controlled effects of light and – like his great mentor, Luis Barragán – a sumptuous and uplifting use of colour. Indisputably modern, Legorreta's architecture evokes the emotive values of traditional Mexican morphologies and landscapes.

In its quest for reinvention, recent architecture often finds itself chasing ephemeral novelty rather than engaging with tangible realities. Innovation generated by abstract models is often vulnerable to irrelevance and misdirection. Regionalism as a source of invention represents the possibility of achieving responsible and eloquent building that constantly renews itself in service to society, a fundamental step in the rehumanization of architecture.

1 William Curtis, 'Towards an Authentic Regionalism', *MIMAR* 19 (January–March 1986), p 24
2 Kenneth Frampton, *Modern Architecture: A Critical History* (London: Thames & Hudson, 1997), p 314
3 Goran Schildt, *Alvar Aalto, The Early Years* (New York: Rizzoli, 1984), p 102

2.00 Pershing Square
Ricardo Legorreta's much-needed green lung in downtown Los Angeles combines hard landscaping with geometric forms and water with vivid colour. The square evokes and reinterprets traditional Hispanic precedents in a sophisticated and modern way.

2.11

2.12

2.13

2.14

Antoine Predock

Frontier Pragmatism

2.10

Architecture in the remote American Southwest reflects natural and man-made landscapes. Underlying physical responses to climate and geography are cultural legacies and memories of the region's pattern of settlement; first by Native Americans and later by waves of Spanish and English colonization. Influences range from elemental Anasazi (a prehistoric tribe famous for its communal buildings) dwellings to the extravagant twentieth-century ephemera of cowboy-movie scenography. Within this diverse terrain, Antoine Predock attempts to merge an image of the district's surreal topography with an evocation of its complex cultural ancestry to form an architecture that reaches beyond historicism and regionalism. 'Every city and landscape involves a sense of place and history, which gives it power', he says, 'I relate to the desert, the commercial strip and everything in-between.'[1]

Based in Albuquerque, New Mexico, Predock has distanced himself geographically and philosophically from the entrenched theoretical positions of America's East and West Coasts. Yet he is not a native of the region. Born in Lebanon, Missouri, in 1936, he was drawn to Albuquerque by what he terms the 'lure of the West' in his late teens. A prolific sketch-artist since childhood, the urge to document his surroundings did not immediately suggest a career in the arts. For the first two years at the University of New Mexico in the late 1950s he studied engineering and went on to take a technical drawing course with Don Schlegel, professor of architecture. Schlegel's passion for his subject inspired Predock to become part of the first generation of students to attend the university's newly established School of Architecture.

One of his earliest influences was Frank Lloyd Wright, whose maniacal intensity thrilled and inspired him. Predock shares with Wright an almost spiritual reverence for the land, along with the confidence and optimism that Wright felt for America. During his apprenticeship in Texas with Charles Adams, a former Wright associate, Predock was exposed to the fanatical Wrightian pursuit of detail that grows gradually and organically from a larger idea.

Following a final year of study at Columbia University's graduate school and an exploration of Spain on a travel fellowship, Predock settled briefly in San Francisco, during which period he absorbed the influence of a variety of artists, including the choreographer Anne Halprin. Intrigued by her attempts to blur the distinction between random and planned movements, Predock strove to create similarly spontaneous compositions. His choreographic experiments gave him an awareness of the physicality of architecture and how the human body moves through and relates to buildings.

Such methodologies continued to intrigue Predock after his return to Albuquerque in 1963. He attributes his lack of a signature style to the models of indeterminacy set by Halprin and such avant-garde composers as John Cage. Beyond providing a forum for his own research, these extradisciplinary studies helped Predock to distance himself from a more conventional historicizing approach to architecture, a necessary detachment he playfully sums up in the assertion 'I have always been more interested in Ray Bradbury than in Andrea Palladio'.[2]

While Predock's buildings remain consistently sparse, planar and primal, they are richly inflected by ideas and images from a plethora of sources ranging from folklore to cyberspace. He is a classic polymath and his career has been characterized by a receptiveness to different experiences and a fascination with cultural marginalia, which he employs as a poetic filter to stimulate his fecund imagination. His scrutiny of what he loosely refers to as 'urban patterns' transcends the city grid to include geological formations and subcultural obsessions, providing him with an unusually wide frame of reference. Popular culture, kitsch, tourist trinkets, B-movies and high art are all treated as equally important sources of inspiration.

Eager to capture and synthesize every possible aspect of site and programme, he diligently records buildings and landscapes through various media – drawing, collage, photography, models and, more recently, video. His travel sketches and conceptual drawings brim with energy and vigour. During the early stages of design, small clay models are used to record quick, impulsive gestures that are translated into the powerful body language of his buildings.

For all his worldly and tangential references, Predock still draws most deeply on the indigenous architectural culture of the Southwest. Enclosed by low horizontal walls, traditional buildings tend to be massive and hermetic, rooted to the earth. Violent seasonal and diurnal extremes of temperature, coupled with severe dust storms encouraged the development of protective, huddled settlements. The magically variable desert light alternately dramatizes and modulates these stark forms. Beyond the sheltering walls, internal spaces are manipulated to create shady passages and patios for year-round use.

Predock's work, like that of Wright and Aalto, is most concerned with site and programme. One of his earliest projects, La Luz Townhouses on the edge of Albuquerque (1967–74), reveals Predock's affinity with the landscape and building forms of the region. At a time when unoriginal modernist apartment blocks were being constructed all over Europe and the United States, La Luz was focused around open space and community planning. Conceived as an oasis in the desert, the complex incorporates a network of lawns, trees, fountains and courtyards, with sweeping views toward the distant Sandia Park. The terracotta colouring and softness of low adobe walls makes the buildings appear to grow out of the earth and evokes connections with the Puebloan people, who were inhabitants of the region. In its concern to 'touch the earth lightly', La Luz represents a decisive rejection of modernism's dehumanizing, functional imperative.

Predock's early reputation was built on a series of family houses and modest institutional buildings. The completion of the Fuller Residence outside Phoenix in 1986 marked the emergence of a bolder, more extrovert style. The house is essentially a collection of pyramids, plazas and pavilions, from which the owners watch the sun rise and set over the desert. Here, the conventional relationship between rooms is transformed into a procession from season to season, earth to sky, matter to spirit. Infused with a sense of theatre and mysticism, the Fuller Residence set the stage for later projects.

Returning from a one-year fellowship at the American Academy in Rome in 1985, Predock devoted his energies to securing larger commissions through competitions. In rapid succession he won the Nelson Fine Arts Center at Arizona State University (1985–89, p 32),

the American Heritage Center and Art Museum at the University of Wyoming (1986–93) and the Las Vegas Library and Children's Museum (1986–90). Predock's definition of architecture as a 'surrogate land form'[3] becomes more evident through the expanded scale of such projects, as does his ability to adapt his shifting mosaic of symbolic references to specific sites and contexts. For instance, the American Heritage Center is dominated by a cone-shaped archive building, like a volcano, pyramid or ancient helmet dramatically erupting from the prairie; the enormous angular forms of the Las Vegas Library resemble sculpted rock formations thrust toward the distant horizon.

Despite his lyrical and imaginative approach to design, Predock is no sentimentalist. The often stark, brooding quality of his architecture is meant to portray the harshness of the desert landscape. As he says, 'The desert is about power and loneliness. The desert is not cute.'[4] His Ventana Vista Elementary School near Tucson (1992–94) has a deliberately blocky, muscular aspect that could be described as frontier pragmatism. Simple forms combined with basic materials (stucco and concrete blocks) make the most of a limited budget.

Predock's jumps in scale and complexity in his buildings have also been accompanied by a wider geographical reach. His site-sounding approach has been applied to several projects in California, including the Mandell Weiss Forum in San Diego (1991) focused around a mirrored glass wall that reflects the site, and the much larger Civic Arts Plaza in Thousand Oaks (1994).

As architectural practice becomes more narrowly focused, Predock's intensely personal vision offers the possibility of a genuinely timeless architecture, unencumbered by the transience of fashionable theories. His kaleidoscopic readings of the world tap into a deep reservoir of human emotions, yet his work maintains a fundamental simplicity and directness. More specifically, in its attachment to land and place, Predock's architecture is quintessentially American, forming part of a tradition that stretches back through Wright and Whitman to Jefferson and the Anasazi. He is energized by the soul of his country and celebrates it through his buildings, extending architecture's spiritual and symbolic range.

1 Antoine Predock, 'Reinterpreting Regionalism: New Mexico', *Architecture* (March 1984), p 120
2 Antoine Predock, 'Out of Albuquerque', *Architectural Record* (October 1988), p 88
3 Ibid.
4 Antoine Predock, 'Desert Education', *Architecture* (March 1995), p 88

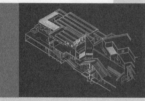

2.1

Nelson Fine Arts Center

Tempe, Arizona, 1985–89

Housing performance, exhibition and teaching areas, Antoine Predock's Fine Arts Center for Arizona State University in Tempe infuses a sprawling campus with a sense of drama and dynamism. The focus of the complex is a large museum containing the university's art collection, while other facilities include a 500-seat proscenium theatre, teaching spaces for dance and theatre arts and two design studios.

By placing the building on the main campus artery of Mill Avenue, Predock reinforces the public edge of the campus started by Frank Lloyd Wright's Gammage Auditorium to the south. The ceremonial entrance establishes a sequence of axial movements through the site, and the dominant metaphor of an oasis in the desert is supported in the transition from blind enclosing walls that define the building's public face to an internal landscape of secret courtyards and arcades. The art museum contains the most public and dramatic spaces, with five galleries and three sculpture courts stacked on three levels. Stairwells are finished in lavender-coloured stucco and are illuminated unevenly from clerestory windows, to spellbinding effect. Other campus buildings can be glimpsed as edited fragments through small openings in the huge walls, throwing up tantalizing vistas.

Inspired by the way in which the mountain ranges of the Sonoran Desert relate to the landscape, Predock explores the traditional Spanish notion of *sol y sombre* (sun and shadow) introducing massing and colour that changes with the angle and intensity of the sun. The building's low silhouette is broken by towers and projections analogous to the forms of the surrounding mountains and buttes.

Turtle Creek House
Dallas, Texas, 1987–93

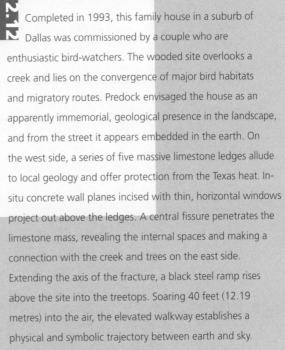

2.12 Completed in 1993, this family house in a suburb of Dallas was commissioned by a couple who are enthusiastic bird-watchers. The wooded site overlooks a creek and lies on the convergence of major bird habitats and migratory routes. Predock envisaged the house as an apparently immemorial, geological presence in the landscape, and from the street it appears embedded in the earth. On the west side, a series of five massive limestone ledges allude to local geology and offer protection from the Texas heat. In-situ concrete wall planes incised with thin, horizontal windows project out above the ledges. A central fissure penetrates the limestone mass, revealing the internal spaces and making a connection with the creek and trees on the east side. Extending the axis of the fracture, a black steel ramp rises above the site into the treetops. Soaring 40 feet (12.19 metres) into the air, the elevated walkway establishes a physical and symbolic trajectory between earth and sky.

The arrival area and entry fissure split the house into two zones. The south wing is a realm of formal social gatherings, while the north wing is the domain where everyday life unfolds. Spread over three levels, the interior is characterized by organizational complexity and surprise, with many different routes through the dramatic, luminous volumes. Each room has access to an outdoor space, and tall glass walls on the largely transparent east side emphasize the house's intimate relationship with the natural world. The topographic roofscape also becomes a habitable zone for al fresco dining and entertaining. Nestled into its sloping site, the building is a hybrid structure, with in-situ concrete retaining walls and floors on the lower two levels, and lighter, steel-and-timber-framed pavilions above.

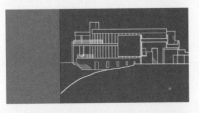

Arizona Science Center
Phoenix, Arizona, 1990–97

2.13

The site for the Arizona Science Center in Phoenix presented Predock with a range of urban contexts, from historic houses to a bustling shopping district, framed by the mountain ranges of the Sonoran Desert. Rejecting the techno-scientific, image-generation potential of the programme, Predock chose to evoke the cosmos through the brooding power and presence of land. The introverted, black-box volumes of five exhibition halls, a theatre and a planetarium are coalesced into a man-made landscape of quasi-natural forms that echoes the topography of the American Southwest. Abstracting the fractal geometries of nature, the science centre appears as a concrete agglomeration of terraces, cliffs, plateaux, mounds and peaks, embodying a primordial, geological potency. A monumental, aluminium-clad wedge cuts through the plan on an east-west axis, uniting the bold composition.

Sunken courts edit out the distracting blare of the city by generating upward views and connecting with the sky above. The processional route through the museum begins with a descent underground to the subterranean entrance courtyard, then moves into the lobby and orientation space adjoining an internal courtyard. The cool, shadowy volume is animated by striations of diffused light and the sensuous play of water. From here, visitors continue to the exhibition space and theatre along a wide corridor between the main volumes.

The promenade concludes in an external courtyard located above the planetarium, where slots in the concrete walls offer panoramic views of the city. Visitors are not merely passive users of the museum, but actively engage with it. Predock's synthesis of form, space and light draws in the elements and creates a powerful affinity with the building's desert surroundings.

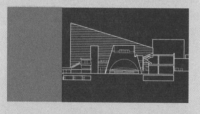

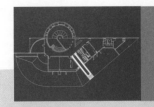

2.14

Rio Grande Nature Center
Albuquerque, New Mexico, 1978–82

The Rio Grande Nature Center on the edge of Albuquerque is a symbol of a profoundly important but rapidly diminishing New Mexico ecosystem. The open fields that border the Rio Grande are vestiges of a pastoral landscape that once stretched the length of the city. The site's natural wetlands are rich in flora and fauna and form a powerful contrast with the semi-arid landscapes of the upland mesas. Acquisition of the site by the state of New Mexico presented an opportunity to maintain important connections between the city, the river and the wildlife reserve.

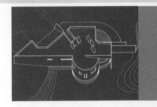

Antoine Predock was commissioned to develop a masterplan for the 170-acre (68.85-hectare) site together with an exhibition building. Set in a cottonwood grove on the edge of a lake, the nature centre takes the form of an introverted hide, affording visitors discreet panoramic views of the wildfowl reserve. Seen from the main approach, the elemental structure blends unobtrusively into the wooded landscape. Walls of rough-formed concrete are minimally articulated by a handful of glazed openings and Predock inventively appropriates industrial materials, for example, a giant corrugated-steel drainage culvert forms and frames an entrance tunnel.

Acknowledging the river's environmental and symbolic significance, water permeates the building's interior. A row of water-filled tubes encircles a sunken ramped exhibition and viewing area. Light delicately shimmers through the tubes from skylights, creating a surreal, underwater effect in the soft gloom of the interior. The ramp descends through the space to allow views of the vast forage areas, the marshlands and a reverse-periscope underwater image of the lake. At each stage along the sloping path, interpretative displays augment the vistas.

Deferring to the beauty of its surroundings yet still asserting a powerful presence in the landscape, this bare concrete building represents a rare instance of nature and architecture in mutual accord.

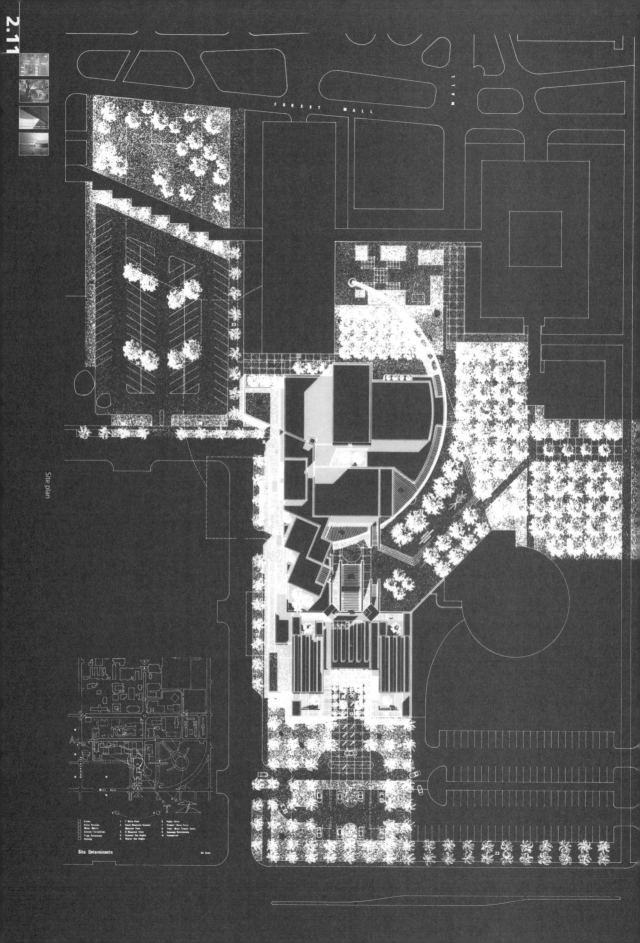

Site plan

FOREST MALL

MALL

Site Determinants

No Scale

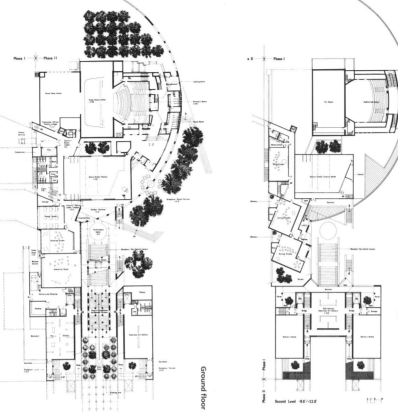

Phase I — Phase II

Phase II

Ground floor

e II — Phase I

Phase I

Phase II

Second Level -9.0'/-22.0'

First floor

2.11 Nelson Fine Arts Center
Many of Predock's morphological metaphors evoke a desert history and topography, but he also sustains an affection for American pop culture. During the evening, the blank wall of the main theatre fly tower is magically mutated into a movie screen, with images projected onto its surface from the

2.11 Nelson Fine Arts Center
With its dense, muscular
collection of angular volumes,
canyonlike spaces and hermetic
walls, the complex evokes the
rugged desert topography.
Around the main performance
and teaching areas is a secret
world of linked courts and
arcades.

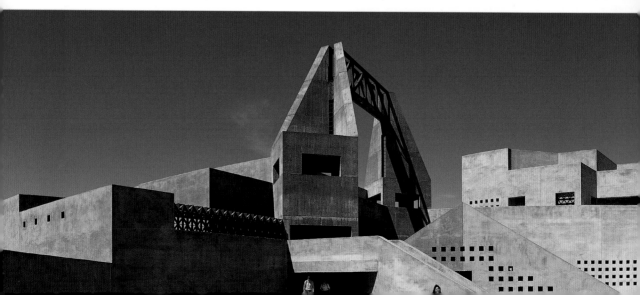

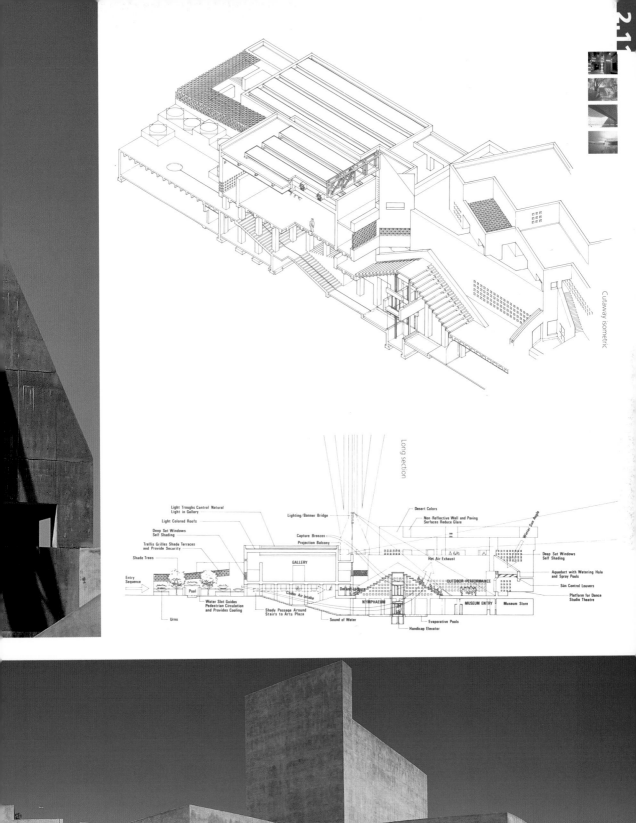

Cutaway isometric

Long section

Light Troughs Control Natural
Light in Gallery
Light Colored Roofs
Deep Set Windows
Self Shading
Trellis Grilles Shade Terraces
and Provide Security
Shade Trees

Lighting/Banner Bridge

Capture Breezes
Projection Balcony

Desert Colors

Non-Reflective Wall and Paving
Surfaces Reduce Glare

Deep Set Windows
Self Shading

Water Spray Angle

GALLERY

Hot Air Exhaust

OUTDOOR PERFORMANCE

Entry
Sequence

Pool

Cooler Air Intake

Dining Lobbies

Aqueduct with Watering Hole
and Spray Pools

Sun Control Louvers

Platform for Dance
Studio Theatre

Water Slot Guides
Pedestrian Circulation
and Provides Cooling

Shady Passage Around
Stairs to Arts Plaza

NYMPHAEUM

Sound of Water

MUSEUM ENTRY

Museum Store

Urns

Evaporative Pools

Handicap Elevator

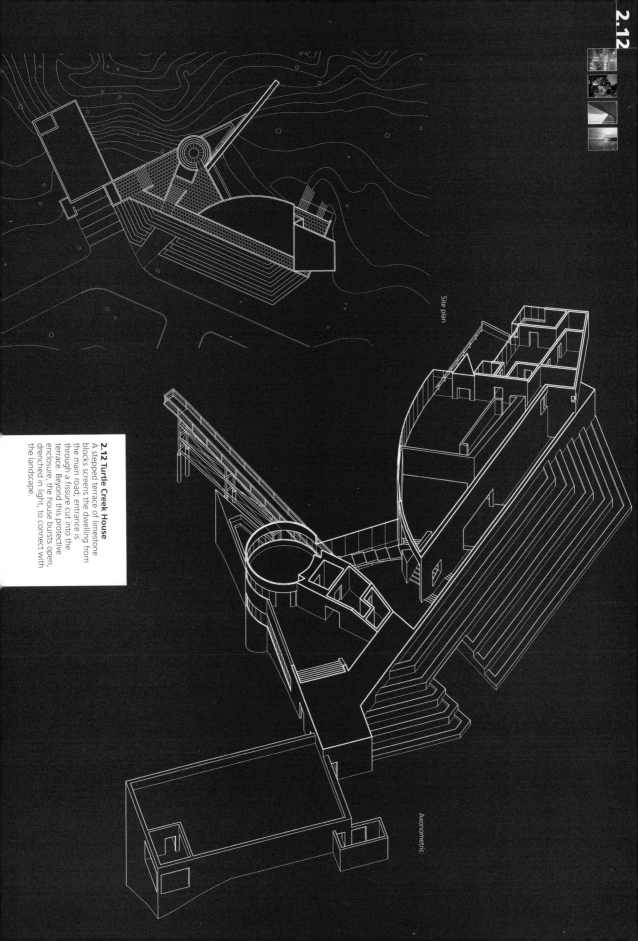

Site plan

2.12 Turtle Creek House
A stepped terrace of limestone blocks screens the dwelling from the main road; entrance is through a fissure cut into the terrace. Beyond this protective enclosure, the house bursts open, drenched in light, to connect with the landscape.

Axonometric

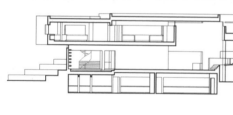

Long section

2.12 Turtle Creek House
Sections show the intricacy of
spatial organization and changes
of level. The interior of the house
is a sequence of airy, luminous
volumes, dominated by the
presence of nature. Mirrored
glass on part of the north
elevation bolsters the illusion of
the building dissolving into the
landscape.

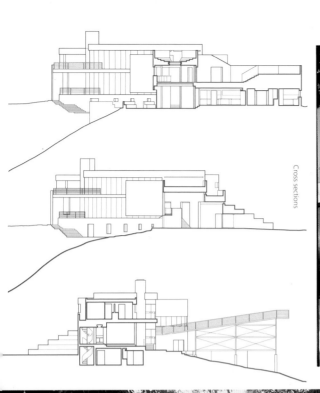

Cross sections

2.13 Arizona Science Center
Above the Science Center's planetarium, an octagonal courtyard frames vistas of the surrounding city. It marks the end of a walk through the museum that begins below ground and culminates in a celebration of the sky. Building down, Predock forces views up and establishes the elemental terms of his architecture.

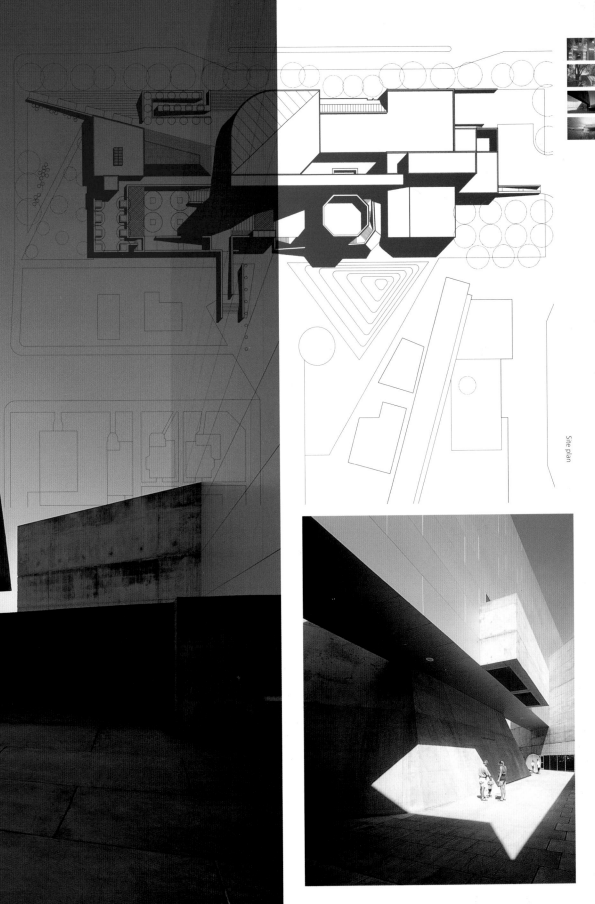

Site plan

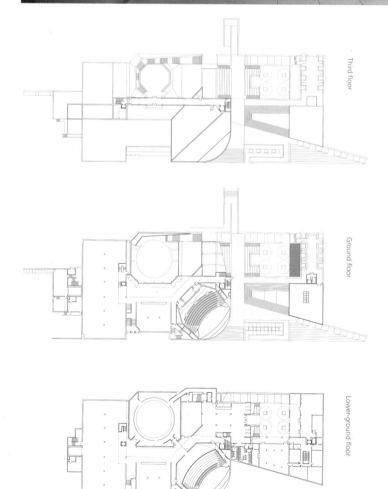

Third floor

Ground floor

Lower-ground floor

2.13

2.13 Arizona Science Center
The building's exuberance is inspired by the specific nature of desert topography and landscape. Bold geometry combines with stark materiality, and although the scale is at times monumental, Predock humanizes and animates the internal exhibition spaces. The section shows the octagonal sky court above the planetarium. Even in the most alien of urban settings, Predock roots his buildings in land and sky.

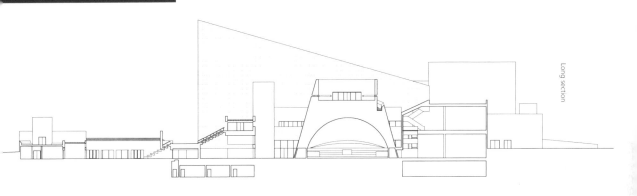

Long section

2.14 Rio Grande Nature Center
Marking Predock's move away from the cosy 'puebloid modern' of his early career, the Nature Center explores a tougher, almost industrial aesthetic, rooted in the region's landscape. The simple structure in the form of a bunker sits unassumingly in its wooded surroundings and offers expansive views over the wildfowl reserve.

Plan

Site plan

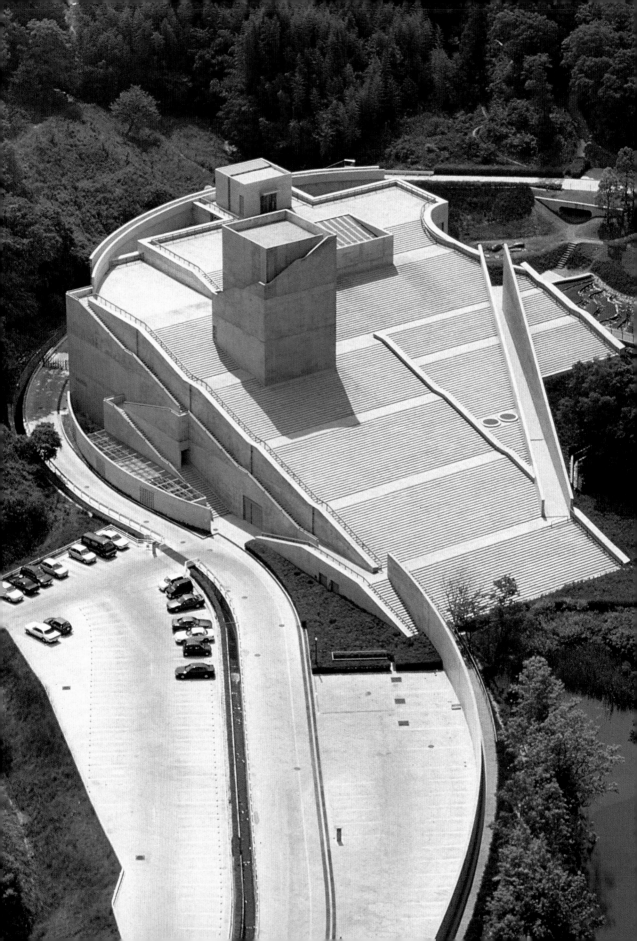

2.21

2.22

2.23

2.24

Tadao Ando
The Realm of *Wabi*

Set against contemporary urban conditions of sensory chaos, visual saturation and transient pleasures, Tadao Ando's architecture embraces a contemplative, ascetic realm of stillness and abstraction. Monastic in their rigour and plainness, his buildings embody a rare mastery of light and materials that seeks to reconnect mankind with nature. Throughout his thirty-year career, Ando has consistently asserted that architecture must be more than an autonomous art form and must strive to enrich the human spirit. Yet the lucidity of such a proposition belies the complex interaction of concepts and concerns that underscore the superficial simplicity of his buildings.

The most powerful influence on Ando's work remains the traditional architecture of his own country. As a child, he came into contact with the great classics of *minka* (farm buildings) and historic Japanese *sukiya* (tea houses). However, the outcome is not a slavish recreation of vernacular forms or styles: instead, Ando reinterprets traditional architecture's immemorial, elemental aspects, such as the effect of light, minimal materiality and man's relationship with nature. Paradoxically, Japanese architecture exerted a similarly profound influence on early European modernists, who saw the simplicity and spatial egalitarianism of traditional Japanese structures as an alternative to hierarchically compartmentalized and ornamented Western buildings. Ando's work also has clear affinities with modernism – especially that of Le Corbusier and Louis Kahn – but he laments the loss of humanity, intimacy and connection with the individual, which resulted from modernism's search for a hypothetical universality. To his austere buildings Ando brings *genus loci* or spirit of place, which explores and responds to the individual qualities and the regional vernacular of each site, so rooting his buildings in both the universal and the particular.

Another important key to understanding Ando's capacity for abstraction is found in the evolution of Japanese aesthetics. In Kansai province during the sixteenth century, the great warlord Toyotomi Hideyoshi and his protégé, tea master Sen no Rikyu, originated the discipline of *wabi* – a strict adherence to the virtues of simplicity, poverty and modesty, in direct opposition to the vulgar ostentation of wealth. It also connotes dissatisfaction with institutional power and resistance to tyranny. Frustrated by the unresponsive worlds of commerce and politics, the artist-intellectual can create his own universe within the realm of *wabi*, governed by self-discipline and ascetic refinement. Osaka, Kansai's provincial capital, is Tadao Ando's native city, so both by birth and inclination, he belongs to this still living tradition, as do many of his clients.

Throughout his career, Ando has explored three basic typologies – houses, temples and museums – set largely in Japan. A handful of overseas projects – the Japanese Gallery at the Art Institute of Chicago (1992), the meditation space for UNESCO (Paris, 1995) and the seminar house for Vitra (Basel, 1993) – also reflect Japan, albeit at a distance. Ando lives and works in the dense, chaotic city of Osaka, where the pressures and flux of modern urban life seem constantly on the verge of overwhelming the inhabitants. Set against this alienating landscape, Ando's buildings are microcosmic enclaves of tranquillity, where the simplest and most basic human activities assume a poetic resonance. In 1969 he set up in practice in the city and four years later, designed a small concrete-walled house in Oyodo, which later became his own atelier. Since Ando began his career, architecture has embraced an often bewildering stylistic plurality, yet his architectural language, approach and thoughts have remained consistent. Any formal or conceptual variations take place within a strict theoretical framework established with the Azuma House, completed in 1976. It is revealing that despite many, often larger, subsequent commissions, this work is still widely considered his representative building.

Slotted into a row of traditional wooden houses in the Sumiyoshi district of Osaka, the tiny Azuma House occupies an area of less than 648 square feet (60 square metres). Measured by Western standards of comfort, it is both inhospitable and impractical. However unlike Western cultures, where the worlds of man and nature are considered separate, Japanese society regards them as intertwined. In the unrelieved harshness of the Azuma House's urban context, Ando has sought to internalize nature. While the windowless perimeter walls exclude the outside world, their purpose is also to capture and to include nature as an inescapable part of the inhabitants' lives. In their almost intimidating plainness and connection with the natural world, Ando's buildings propose a provocative alternative vision of human existence.

The principal tangible component of Ando's architecture is the wall, enlivened and transformed by light. His revival of the wall as a fixed, containing element coupled with the rejection of open, universal space is another important divergence from conventional modernist doctrines. In dwellings, such as the Nakayama House (1985) and the Kidosaki House (1986), the wall acts as a demarcation of territory, both separating and joining inhabitant and surroundings. Standing independently, as at the Naoshima Art Museum (1992), the wall sweeps through the landscape, emphasizing the polarity between the natural and the man-made.

With occasional exceptions – notably the majestic, iroko-clad Japanese Pavilion for the Seville Expo (1992) and the Museum of Wood (Hyogo, 1994) – Ando's walls display little material variation. Fabricated from exquisitely smooth poured concrete, the walls are physically static and permanent. Considerable care is taken to ensure that they are as perfect as manufacturing techniques allow. The formula for Ando's concrete is a surprisingly standard specification, with the emphasis placed on supervision and the technical capabilities of the construction team. In reality, while the walls are finished to a remarkably high standard, they often bear the traces of successive pours. Just as the *raku* potter relies on the unpredictable nature of the kiln to create serendipitous designs and textures, Ando relishes the unexpected flaws and changes in character that can result from the pour. But he also regards concrete as an ordinary substance formed, moulded and finished by the manual skill of building workers. Exposed shuttering based on the size of traditional *tatami* mats (6 x 2.99 feet, 1.83 x 0.91 metres) is often used as a basic template, alluding to the modularized nature of Japanese domestic architecture and exemplifying Ando's reinvention of the vernacular.

Immaculately crafted and generally lacquered with a protective coating, the luminous sheen of the concrete walls imparts a strangely ethereal delicacy that contradicts their robustness. When animated by changing light, the material assumes the sublime potency of mass altered by nature. As Ando poetically describes it 'The way I employ concrete it lacks sculpturesque solidity and weight. It serves to produce light, homogeneous surfaces. I treat concrete as a cool, inorganic material with a concealed background of strength. My intent is not to express the nature of the material itself, but to employ it to establish the single intent of the space.'[1]

Although Ando's career has been characterized by consistency, there have been some detectable shifts, particularly with regard to scale and context. Since the time of the Raika Headquarters (1989), his work has become less introverted and hermetic. Sensitively proportioned concrete apparitions rise up before expanses of green landscape or open sea: observation towers for the contemplation of nature. The Chikatsu-Asuka Historical Museum (1990–94, p 60) is transformed into a monumental stepped terrace poised above fields of ancient burial mounds.

This reading of and response to context has born fruit with a major foreign commission. In 1997, Ando won an international competition for the new Museum of Modern Art at Fort Worth in Texas. A series of oblong exhibition halls reflects the roofline of the adjacent Kimbell Museum by Louis Kahn, one of Ando's great mentors. Here the concrete is surrounded by a glass skin, exploring the beauty and potential of a new material. Ando is now established on the world stage, yet in its sense of quiet authenticity, his work remains true to Japan. Like Katsushika Hokusai's (a famous Japanese print-maker, 1760–1849) bridges that lead away into the mists and the unknown, Ando's buildings invite us on a succession of tantalizing internal journeys. His is an architecture of intensity, lyricism and timelessness, qualities evoked and celebrated by Japanese artist and author Yasunari Kawabata: 'He walked contemplating the lake; it seemed that the reflected images would continue forever and never separate'.[2]

1 'Rokko Housing', *Quadrini di Casabella* (1986), p 62
2 Yasunari Kawabata quoted in *Casabella* (no 558, June 1989), p 59

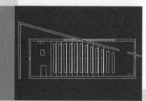

Church of the Light
Ibaraki, Japan, 1987–89

Located in a quiet residential suburb to the northeast of Osaka, the Church of the Light is a stark concrete container. Oriented toward the sun and the adjacent pastor's residence, the triple-cube volume is bisected at 15 degrees by a freestanding wall that defines the chapel's central body and its triangular entrance hall. Although the church is fairly compact – no larger than a modest house – it is used for classical concerts, community meetings and Christian services.

The texture of the concrete is perhaps not quite as immaculately finished as some of Ando's more recent buildings (because of cost limitations), but it nevertheless produces the illusion of a taut, tensile surface rather than a heavy, earthbound mass. The austere external enclosure provides a frame that isolates the sacred space from its immediate surroundings, while the cool concrete walls inside are set off by floors and pews fabricated from stained-timber planks.

The main source of light is a dramatic, cruciform opening incised into the east wall behind the chancel. This is supplemented by two full-height openings – where the diagonal blade of concrete slices through the side of the building – which soften the contrast between the radiant light of the cross and the introspective, sepulchral interior.

The cross is rich in symbolism; allied to light, representing the divine, the expression of the cross as an opening in the wall elevates it to a communion with heaven. It becomes a door to the realm above, through which the gods may descend to earth and man may ascend to heaven. In this calm sanctuary, human spirit, nature and the godlike are joined in a cosmic union of space and light.

Chikatsu-Asuka Historical Museum
Minami Kawachi, Japan, 1990–94

2.22

The southern part of the Osaka prefecture contains a remarkable aggregation of ancient Japanese burial mounds (*kofun*), dating from the fifth and sixth centuries. Ando was asked to design a centre for exhibiting and researching *kofun* culture that transcends the scope of the conventional museum and acts as a focus for both excavated objects and the surrounding clusters of tumuli, which remain largely undisturbed in their original settings.

Like a Mayan temple emerging from the deepest jungle, the structure has a brooding, monolithic presence. The immense concrete slope of the roof is paved with rough cobbles of local white *mikage* granite and can also be used for a variety of outdoor activities – drama and musical performances, lectures and festivals.

The entrance to the complex below is indicated by a long cryptic path cut at an angle into the staircase. Enclosed by walls of smooth concrete, the oppressively narrow route emerges next to the projecting cube of the entrance. From the brilliantly light entrance hall, there is a slow and symbolic descent into metaphorical and literal darkness by means of a curving ramp. The most prominent item on display in the exhibition space on the lower level is a giant model of a burial complex. Dimly lit cases of artifacts line the walls.

The manner in which the sequence of spaces and events has been fused constitutes more than a simple museum visit: it is a mystical progress concerned with the essential nature of man and his place in the world.

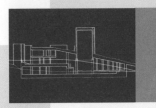

Meditation Space, UNESCO
Paris, 1994–95

2.23 In 1995 UNESCO celebrated its fiftieth anniversary. As the organization's aim is to promote peace through educational, scientific and cultural activities, director-general Frederico Mayor suggested commemorating the anniversary with a meditation space on the same site as Marcel Breuer's iconic headquarters. The new space is envisaged as a place to pray and meditate for peace, a neutral haven where religious, ethnic, cultural and historical differences have no place.

Lying next to Isamu Noguchi's Japanese garden, Ando's building is a cylindrical, one-storey structure, a mere 356.4 square feet (33 square metres) in area. The cylinder is bisected by a slightly raised walkway that links up with a system of ramps leading to other parts of the UNESCO complex. Executed in fairfaced concrete, the building is a distilled expression of pure Euclidean form; stripped of adornment, there are just two bald apertures where the walkway slices through the building.

Inside, light is diffused into the cylinder through a narrow strip of skylight that runs around the roof's perimeter. A contemplative quiescence pervades the solemn, minimal space. With the cooperation of the city of Hiroshima, granite that was exposed to radiation from the atomic bomb is used to pave the floor. Despite the sad fact that not a single day has passed without an armed conflict raging in some part of the world since the Second World War, this small haven of spiritual tranquillity affirms a belief in the human capacity for peaceful coexistence.

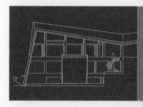

Hompukuji Water Temple
Awaji Island, Japan, 1989–91

Nestling on a hill overlooking Osaka Bay, the Hompukuji Water Temple is a radical challenge to the centuries-old conventions governing Buddhist temple design in Japan. In form, materials and processional sequence, Ando's contemporary building is far removed from traditional timber structures. The temple hall is placed underground, beneath a large pool filled with luxuriant floating lotus plants. In Buddhist iconography, the lotus signifies the enlightened soul rising from the world's corruptions and suggests the presence of Amida Buddha, who is believed to bring a heavenly message from the Western Paradise.

Expressed as an impassive, enigmatic volume in the landscape, an elliptical pool is enclosed by curved concrete walls of exquisite smoothness. The subterranean sanctuary is reached by a narrow stairway sliced across the pool's short axis. Visitors process down the long stairway below the level of the water, a potent inversion of the ascent to a conventional temple. The pool's shape is extended below ground as the building's defining shape: geometric forms are nested within each other, suggesting harmony rather than Ando's characteristic imbalance.

Roughly half the ellipse contains a circular temple sanctuary, defined by a wall of tightly lapped Japanese cypress boards. The boards, columns and timber screens enclosing the statue of Amida Buddha are rendered an intense red. Natural light is admitted behind the shrine through windows in the exposed retaining wall where the hill falls away. The improbability of discovering light after descending underground, beneath a pool of water, magnifies the temple's divine drama and mystery.

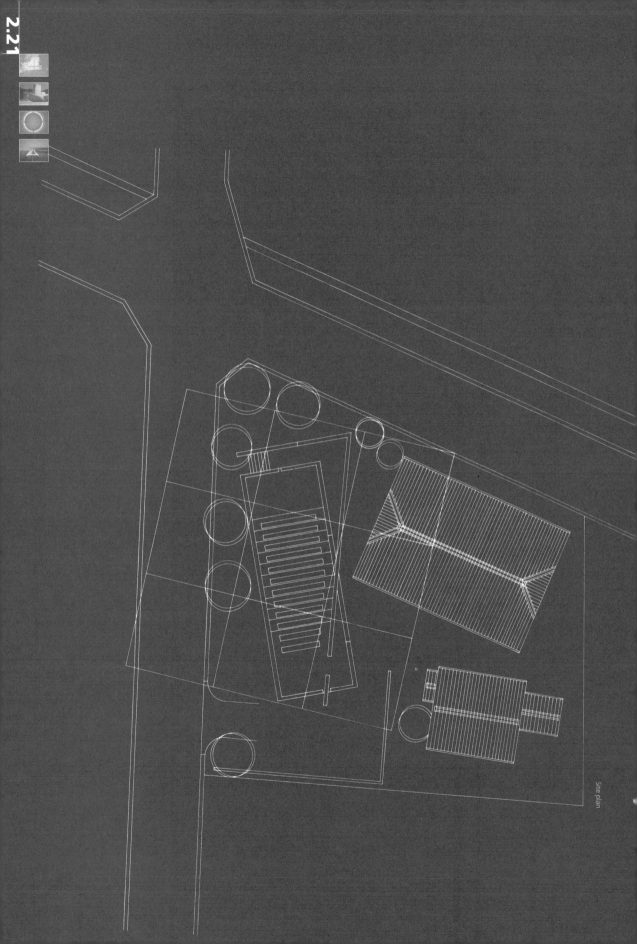

Site plan

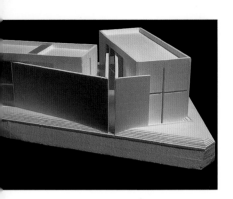

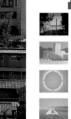

2.21 Church of the Light
Shrouded in greenery within an Osaka suburb, the monolithic façade conceals the graceful articulation of light inside the sanctuary. The massive external walls are made from poured concrete, 1.5 inches (380 millimetres) in thickness, which ensures that quietude is preserved from the outside world.

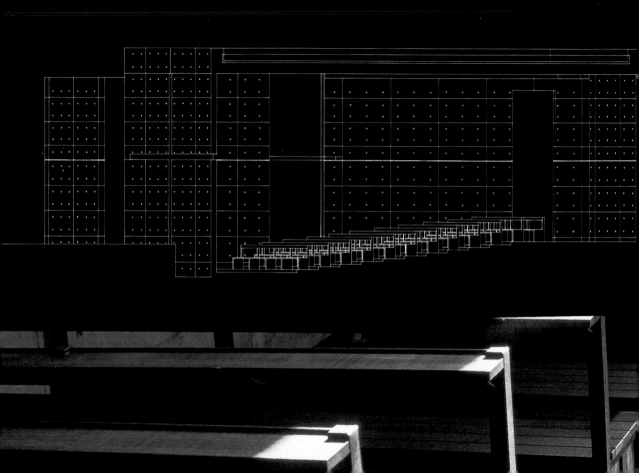

2.22 Chikatsu-Asuka Museum
Set in the rolling hills of the Osaka prefecture, the building's strong sculptural form is an almost organic extension of the landscape, accentuated by its roof, which also functions as a monumental staircase leading to a broad terrace from which to view the nearby tombs.

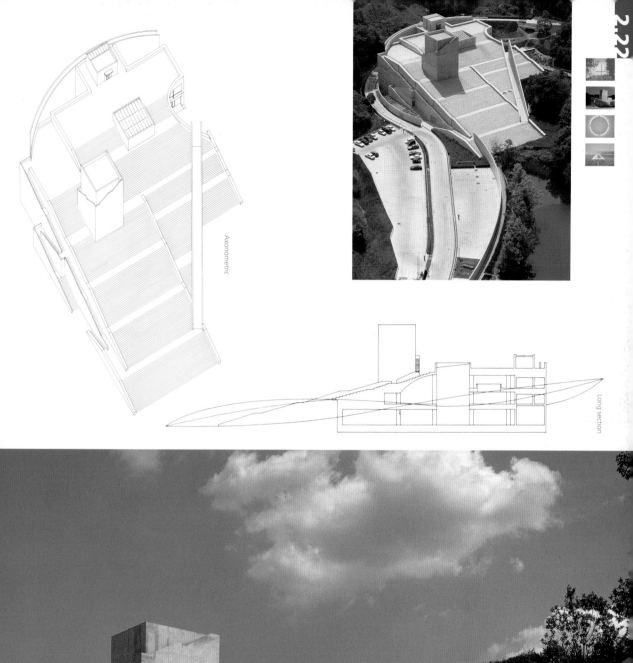

Axonometric

Long section

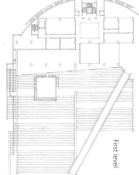

First level

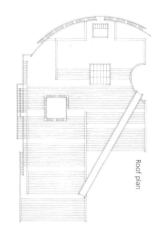

Roof plan

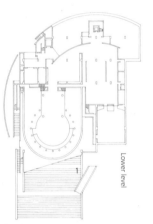

Lower level

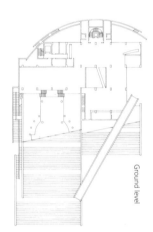

Ground level

2.22 Chikatsu-Asuka Museum
Submerged within the hill, the lower floor's strange keyhole form evokes the distinctive shape of the tumuli and is dominated by a vast model of a burial complex. Conversely, the first floor's design allows light to filter into the exhibition space.

2.23 Meditation Space
Despite the closeness of the other buildings, the minimal space allows the visitor to be detached, both physically and consciously from the surroundings. Its starkness belies the poetic balance between volume and light to induce a sense of well-being and contemplation.

2.24 Hompukuji Water Temple
Set against Osaka Bay in the distance, the site occupies an imposing position. Lotuses, symbolizing the presence of Amida Buddha, cover the surface of the oval-shaped pond, their religious significance is the only clue as to what lies beneath. A dramatically located flight of stairs, which almost cuts the pond in half, gives the visitor the impression of walking on water when descending to the underground temple.

2.24 Hompukuji Water Temple
In contrast to the neutral concrete exterior and gently curving forms, the circular and latticed wooden temple below ground is painted a rich vermilion, a traditional Buddhist colour. This is the first use of strong hue in Ando's monochromatic architecture and creates the illusion of air saturated with colour.

2.31

2.32

2.33

2.34

Wiel Arets
Puritan Abstraction

Wiel Arets belongs to a generation of young Dutch architects seeking to explore new ways of making and thinking about buildings. Defying easy categorization, his architecture is dominated by subtlety and paradox. Where his buildings seem simple, they also reveal great richness and poetry; where they appear concise and lucid, they also leave space for individual imagination. Superficially, Arets displays an affinity with Mies van der Rohe and Giuseppe Terragni, yet he has given his own very particular interpretation to the familiar language of early modern formalism. He is also inspired by a raft of such tangential cultural sources as literature and film, and such diverse and unrelated disciplines as ethnography, philosophy and biology.

Arets has always combined building with theorizing and teaching: he has taught at the Architectural Association in London, New York's Cooper Union and Columbia University. In 1995 he succeeded Herman Hertzberger as director of the Berlage Institute in Amsterdam, which runs the most important internationally oriented postgraduate architecture course in The Netherlands. He has published studies on Casa Malaparte by Italian rationalist Adalberto Libera and on the work of Mexican master Luis Barragán.

Paradoxically, for an architect with such a sophisticated world view, Arets's origins are distinctly provincial. Born in the southern industrial Dutch town of Heerlen in 1955, Arets trained at the Technical University of Eindhoven. Since the mid-1970s, Eindhoven has encouraged wider and more outspoken architectural debate, than other Dutch universities. Arets has subsequently collaborated with Dutch philosopher Eric Bolle and architectural critic Joost Meeuwsen, both of whom studied at Eindhoven.

On leaving Eindhoven, Arets set about expanding his horizons. Study trips to the then Soviet Union and Japan led to the appearance of critical articles in Dutch architectural journals, and a well-received book and exhibition on the Limburg modernist Fritz Peutz. In 1984, he set up in private practice in his native town of Heerlen, located far from traditional Dutch centres of culture, reflecting Arets's inclination to stand neutrally aloof from the neo-modernist mainstream of Dutch architecture; rather than being claimed by any specific place, his work is to a large extent lodged in text.

Arets's projects are consistently accompanied by extensive written descriptions and analyses. These are not so much explanations or justifications, as independent trajectories in words; verbal counterpoints to the visual, exploring the autonomous nature of architecture. Philosophers such as Derrida, Foucault and Baudrillard are summoned to provide theoretical parallels and insights. Through his writing, Arets has drawn Dutch architectural criticism into the higher realm of international debate, where it is seen by some as an invigorating draft of intellectualism in a country of sober, Calvinist practicality.

A number of themes emerge from his text and projects. Arets prefers the suggestiveness of translucency over the false promise of clarity. Through a puritan subversiveness, his work thwarts harmony and reconciliation, instead fomenting conditions of unpredictability and change. In his most recent writing, architecture is seen as virological; it operates invisibly as a catalyst of events.

Arets extends this biological analogy to the function and nature of the city, which he compares to the human body, 'The body is an ensemble of functioning organisms, just as the city may be regarded as an ensemble of functioning buildings. The city requires intervention, transplantation and other surgical insertions brought about by architecture.'[1]

New buildings are effectively cut and implanted into the living organism of the city. Through their analytical response to site and programme, Arets's urban insertions suggest an alternative to conventional solutions.

As in classical temples and minimalist art, his work is not a mimetic, literal obedience to context, but rather an interpretation of it. 'We want our buildings to merge into the existing context, but at the same time to be flexible and open to change',[2] Arets has written. He employs two principle tactics: disappearance and foldability. Both are expressed through the materiality of external skins that act like alabaster – partly transparent and partly translucent – creating a chameleonic reflection of the environment.

Arets's pure geometries and unadorned materiality evoke both artistic and architectural precedents. The distilled forms of early projects such as a fashion shop in Maastricht (1988), with its façade of rusted Corten steel, recall the spare, minimalist sculptures of Donald Judd and Sol Le Witt. His buildings also reflect the influence of contemporary Japanese architecture, notably that of Tadao Ando. Like Ando, Arets demonstrates a concrete hardness, bareness, colourlessness and apparent asceticism. His projects spring to life through a subtle interplay of constantly changing light, ingeniously conceived circulation routes and geometric articulation. Arets purifies space, material and light to a raw essence. However, this should not be dismissed as nihilism, but rather as a kind of abstract elementalism, a stripping away of distracting or superfluous detail. Ando's buildings, especially his houses, clearly set themselves apart from the modern metropolis with all its luxury, comfort and exaggerated consumption. They are monastically austere, with the aim of nurturing a heightened relationship between man and nature. This is achieved by controlling and dramatizing the presence of light, by focusing and framing outward views.

In Arets's Academy of Arts Extension in Maastricht (1989–93, p 80) such parallels are particularly explicit, not only in terms of material (concrete and glass bricks), but also in the way in which light penetrates the main circulation ramp and the elevated walkway linking the two parts of the building. Made from two vertical concrete walls, between which panels of glass brick rise to form the roof and floor, the walkway dramatically soars through the tree tops of the surrounding square. Studios and workshops are located at one end of the bridge while the other end emerges into a roof garden. Not only does this open up vertical access to the building, it also links the functions horizontally, defining a processional *promenade architecturale.*

Reinforced concrete is cast using inventive shuttering techniques to generate different textures; sometimes severe and pure, sometimes coarse and soft (like silk), according to the light raking across its surface. Arets's reinforced concrete refers to its own fabrication; the marks and effects of its temporary generative structure are clearly inherent in the finished building. For instance, at the AZL Pension Fund Headquarters in Heerlen (1990–95, p 92), formwork seams and holes for the spacing pieces create gridded patterns, transformed by repetition into an independent abstract figure.

Inside his buildings, Arets creates taut, orthogonal spaces defined by smooth planes. Materials are connected without explicit construction joints, so they retain their pristine aspect and become sculptural elements. Yet this asceticism is often far from comfortable. The potent, stripped aesthetics of concrete, glass blocks and other raw materials give Arets's interiors the quality of a film or stage set. At the Maastricht Academy of Arts, the fashion studio with its sewing machines and mannequins is reminiscent of a nineteenth-century factory hall; the metal workshop suggests the paintings of Francis Bacon; and the lecture hall recalls a Franciscan monastery. A walk through the building is thus elevated into a ritual experience, infused with phenomenological possibilities.

In the same way that a director turns individual images and scenes into a film by editing, Arets combines programmes, events, materials, vistas and perspectives to generate a complex and resonant architectural experience. As he observes, 'We have come to see the world as a picture. We see things through a car window, from the train or plane; video and television bring pictures into our homes after everything that happens has been translated into images.'[3] For Arets, contemporary technologies and evolving forms of media have conspired to distort our sense of reality, giving rise to new and different ways of seeing things. Space is not merely an emptiness enclosed by walls, but an interval between successive events. His cinematographically inspired vision embraces a subtle but far-reaching game of familiarity and strangeness, idyll and nightmare. As in David Lynch's films, the one can turn into the other at any moment.

Ole Bouman, editor of the influential Dutch architecture magazine *Archis,* encapsulates the paradoxical essence of Arets's architecture. 'These are buildings that turn visitors into *dramatis personae.* Drama is always imminent. Surrealistic effects hasten the process of alienation. A lot of grey, a lot of black, steel, wood, zinc, concrete. A Kafkaesque mystery, a looming menace. Sometimes you see shadows or are they ghosts behind translucent walls or perforated screens? This is hermetic architecture: while you unquestionably feel and experience it, you also remain at a respectful distance.'[4]

1 Wiel Arets, *An Alabaster Skin* (Rotterdam: 010 Publishers, 1992), p 6
2 Josep María Montaner, 'Wiel Arets: European Architecture After Postmodernism', *El Croquis* (no 85, 1997), p 30
3 Wiel Arets, *An Alabaster Skin* (Rotterdam: 010 Publishers, 1992), p 21
4 Ole Bouman, 'Arets Liberales', *El Croquis* (no 85, 1997), p 36

Academy of Arts Extension
Maastricht, The Netherlands, 1989–93

2.31

Maastricht, a former Roman town on the river Meuse, lies close to the border with Germany and Belgium. At its heart is a dense medieval core of ancient brick and limestone houses. Arets was asked to extend the existing Academy of Arts, which lies in the historic part of the town. Prior to Arets's involvement, the area was restructured to a modest urban masterplan by fellow Dutch architects Mecanoo, creating housing and a square, the Hendriksplein.

Arets's building pierces the square, both completing it and disrupting it. A pair of apparently impenetrable blind cubes sit detached and askew in the square, connected by an elevated bridge. The smaller volume houses a lecture theatre, library and cafeteria and is joined to the existing Academy. This has been renovated and its walls plastered black. Between new and old blocks is an interstitial wedge-shaped light well. Circulation around this annexe is by means of a meandering ramp with unexpected views and subtly modulated light.

The second larger volume contains various communal workshops and studios and an external space for the display of sculpture. It is accessible only by the elevated bridge joined to the smaller block. The bridge forms the conceptual heart of the scheme, transforming the building into a monumental gateway to the Hendriksplein. Constructed from raw concrete with a glass-block floor, the bridge brushes the top of an imposing tree, giving it a surreal, sculptural quality.

The new volumes are taut, geometric exercises in formal and material minimalism. The tantalizing surfaces of glass-block walls, framed and inscribed by a Cartesian grid of concrete, suggest the impenetrability of a casket or reliquary, a container as precious and entrancing as its protected contents. Like a veil, the skin of the building is both opaque and transparent, at once enclosing and disclosing; what Arets has referred to in his extensive writings as an 'alabaster skin'. At night, the square is illuminated by the soft glow of the seductively luminous glass walls.

Apartment Blocks
Tilburg, The Netherlands, 1992–94

A former industrial zone along Wilhemina Park in the centre of Tilburg is being transformed into a new cultural and housing district. A former wool factory has been renovated to house the De Pond Museum and its remarkable collection of contemporary art. As part of the area's redevelopment, Arets was asked to design a social-housing scheme. His other housing projects include the towering apartment block on KNSM Island in Amsterdam and flats for the elderly in Maastricht. The Dutch pursue a vigorous social-housing policy, reinforced by imaginative architectural commissioning. Arets is just one example.

Containing sixty-seven apartments for elderly people, Arets's housing is divided into two blocks. One, a V-shaped building, is positioned up against the side of the museum to create an internal courtyard; the other, a linear slab, overlooks the museum garden. Based on accepted standards for contemporary Dutch housing, each apartment is 831.6 square feet (77 square metres), with a living room, bedroom, kitchen and bathroom. The public façade of each block is clad in a rough stucco or *putz*, with internal balconies from which residents can survey the street. The private sides facing the museum garden are made from glass blocks, articulated and defined by a slim concrete frame. Behind this shimmering, translucent skin lies a broad spinal corridor 9.8 feet (3 metres) wide, conceived as a communal space for residents to sit out and chat with each other. Light is modulated and filtered by the glass blocks, creating a calm, softly lit space. At night the effect is reversed when internal lighting from the apartments illuminates the garden and courtyard.

Regional Police Headquarters
Vaals, The Netherlands, 1993–95

2.33 Set in gently rolling countryside, Vaals is a small town at the southern tip of The Netherlands. The regional police force was reorganized to embody a more open way of working and Wiel Arets was commissioned to provide a new building. Arets's design evokes a subtle interplay of familiarity and eccentricity, reflecting the different degrees of openness between the public and the police, but also between the police themselves.

The building is divided into three linear elements, each made of contrasting materials: zinc, timber and concrete. Within this tripartite structure, a series of zones is created with different levels of police and public access. Work and meeting areas for the police are contained in a low-slung concrete slab furthest from the public area. The intermediate timber-clad block houses administrative and technical spaces, while detention cells and interrogation rooms are found in the more prominent zinc-clad volume. The simultaneously public and hermetic character of the building is underscored by the use of translucent glass walls in the interior, which admit light, but not views.

Despite the prosaic, functional brief, Arets exploits the creative possibilities of form and material to the full. With its gently raked roof and chamfered ends, the concrete-coated volume thrusts forward in the landscape, and the timber and zinc cladding form an expressive contrast to this heavy, earthbound mass. For all its diversity, the building has a tectonic coherence, due to consistent economy of detail and the way in which each material relates to and identifies individual volumes.

2.34

AZL Pension Fund Headquarters
Heerlen, The Netherlands, 1990–95

The AZL headquarters in Arets's native town of Heerlen develops the formal and material themes present in the Maastricht Academy of Arts, in which architecture serves to animate a larger social organism. AZL originated with Limburg's coal industry, survived postwar pit closures and re-formed as an insurance and pension firm. Dating from the 1940s, its original head office is in the inner suburbs of Heerlen, occupying a flat slice through a block framed by dense terraces of houses. The new programme includes office accommodation for 220 staff, divided into cellular and open-plan spaces, together with meeting rooms, a café and parking.

The theme governing the project's development is the notion of plugging; in effect the new buildings are plugged into the existing structures. New facilities are housed in an elongated volume that runs perpendicular to the original renovated building. Crisp planes of concrete and stainless steel slide over each other to float above a large linear space carved into the ground. The hovering planes engender a sensation of gravity defiance. The carved volumes function as geometry-adjusting devices, accommodating the entire complex to the subtle misalignment of the streets that define the AZL site. A narrow slab of offices is joined to the main linear volume, plugged in roughly halfway along its length to create the third side of a courtyard between new and old elements.

Inside, the project exhibits an economic logic in its details and fixtures. Black metal components recall the Dessau Bauhaus and office spaces have a functional, workaday spirit, with grey-green carpeting, moveable translucent partitions and storage units that provide acoustic absorption. Elegantly grafted on to the existing building, Arets's new headquarters is an expressively reductivist manipulation of space, light, material and programme.

Site plan

2.31 Academy of Arts Extension
Clad in a translucent skin of glass
blocks, the new extension has a
sober, primal inscrutability with
slotlike windows penetrating the
glass walls. It is linked to the old
building by an enclosed bridge
that forms a gateway to the
urban square.

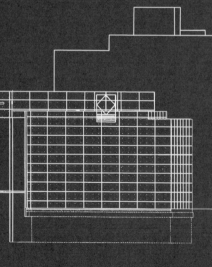

East elevation

2.32 Apartment Blocks, Tilburg
Arets's apartment blocks for elderly people in Tilburg reflect the Dutch state's imaginative commissioning policy with regard to social housing. The cool ascetic language of glass blocks held in a concrete frame makes no concessions to domestic cosiness. Yet despite its apparent formal austerity, the scheme has a quiet, unassuming dignity.

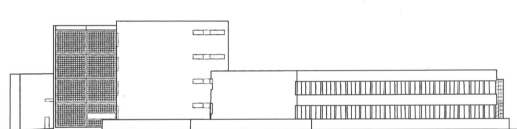

South elevation

2.32 Apartment Blocks, Tilburg
The apartment blocks are exercises in material minimalism. Tall glass-block walls form a glistening surface and create wonderfully peaceful patterns as the light gently diffuses through them.

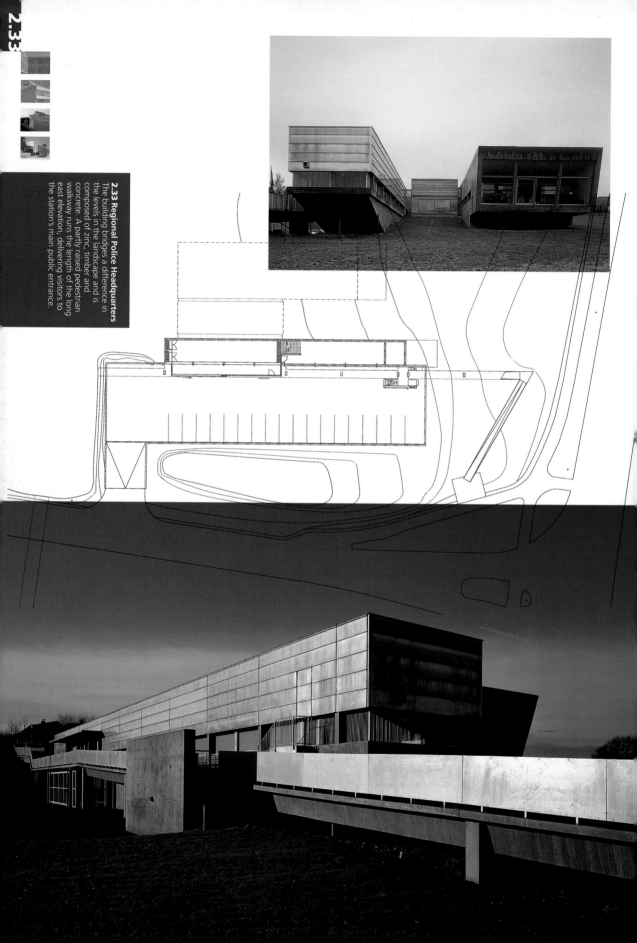

2.33 Regional Police Headquarters
The building bridges a difference in the levels in the landscape and is composed of zinc, timber and concrete. A partly raised pedestrian walkway runs the length of the long east elevation, delivering visitors to the station's main public entrance.

Upper floor

2.33 Regional Police Headquarters
Arets uses translucent and transparent glass screens and walls to create different spaces within the police station. Framed vistas of the surrounding landscape combine with masked and filtered views through the interior to preserve a sense of

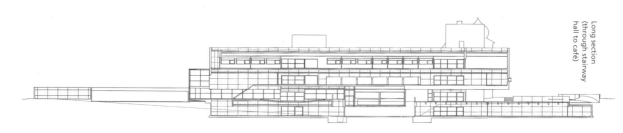

Long section
(through stairway
hall to café)

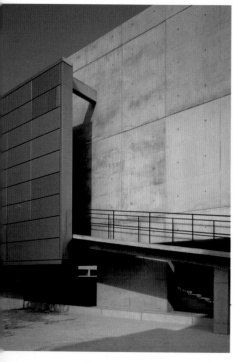

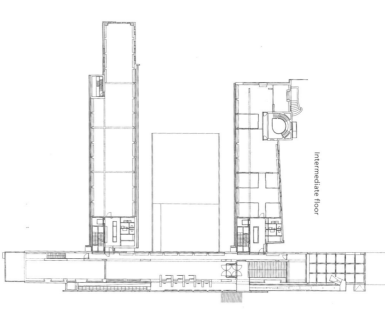

Intermediate floor

2.34 AZL Pension Fund Headquarters

Grafted on to an existing building, the new offices are an expressively reductivist manipulation of space, light and programme. At the main street end, the cantilevered snout of the reception volume is animated by a single strip of glazing that acts as a visor, while at the other end, the glass cube of the staff café overlooks a spreading oak tree.

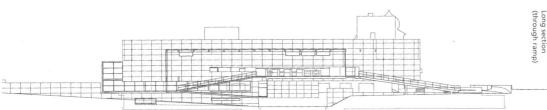

Long section
(through ramp)

Wiel Arets : 93

2.34 AZL Pension Fund Headquarters
Interiors are defined by a series of crisp, orthogonal planes in concrete and glass. Arets's concrete clearly bears the marks of its fabrication, transforming surfaces into independent abstract areas animated by the effects of light. Fixtures and detailing are distinguished by an elegant economy, reflecting a functional yet refined spirit.

2.40 Ricardo Legorreta

2.41 Metropolitan Cathedral
2.42 Contemporary Art Museum
2.43 Pershing Square
2.44 Office Building, Monterrey

2.41

2.42

2.43

2.44

Ricardo Legorreta
Colour and Light

Ricardo Legorreta is Mexico's Mexican architect. His work has evolved out of the patient study and understanding of his country's rich vernacular architectural traditions. Yet Legorreta is not simply an accomplished regionalist, but an architect whose work has universal meaning while rooted in Mexican settings. Legorreta's work poetically embodies this elusive synthesis of local and global.

Mexico has a resonant history, forged by the ancient civilizations of Mesoamerica encountering the sixteenth-century Spanish culture of the colonizing *conquistadores*. What emerged over centuries was a hybrid mixture of the two – a *mestizo* culture – based on diversity, contradiction and the vitality of personal expression. Modern Mexico is imbued with passion, colour, mysticism and a preoccupation with death.

The dichotomy of influences competing with and complementing each other finds potent expression in Legorreta's architecture. Throughout his career Legorreta has been keenly aware that traditional architecture is a spirit to be cherished and not simply a source to be plundered. When visiting rural villages and towns he approaches indigenous buildings with a sense of awe and humility. It is revealing that Legorreta speaks of his appreciation of traditional architecture in terms of principles and lessons, not in terms of forms and motifs. Drawn first-hand from immersion in Mexican life, his architecture reflects an intuitive understanding of his country's remarkable history and culture.

Ricardo Legorreta can trace his family back many generations in Mexico, but his ancestors originated from the town of Legorreta in the Basque region of Spain. He was born into a prominent Mexican family in 1931, where his father encouraged a strong sense of personal discipline and social responsibility. It was a close and deeply religious household, as most Mexican families tend to be, and Legorreta's intense affinity for the spiritual reflects his upbringing.

Despite growing up in the sprawling metropolis of Mexico City, Legorreta was exposed to his country's architecture through regular visits to the countryside, where he explored local villages, haciendas, convents and churches. On completing his studies at the Universidad Nacional Autómena de México in 1952, Legorreta went to work in the studio of José Villagran García, a leading Mexican modernist and influential teacher of architecture. In Europe, the heroic spirit of the modern movement was derived from the potential of new technology, but in Mexico, modernism was more a reflection of social imperative. Villagran embraced the disciplined rationalism of modernism, but his theories also espoused a strong moral dimension. Such pragmatism made a considerable impact on the young Legorreta. 'Architecture should be at the service of great ideals and people, and not at the whim of economics, politics and demagoguery',[1] he once remarked.

In 1960 Legorreta set up in private practice with partners Noé Castro and Carlos Vargas. The office's first major work was the Automex Factory for Chrysler in Toluca (1964), which combined the spatial qualities of Mexican vernacular architecture with geometric, rationalist forms. Underpinning the project was a concern for the dignity and well-being of the workers. At the opening of the factory, Legorreta was introduced to Luis Barragán, who was to prove to be another key figure in his development. Legorreta went on to collaborate with Barragán on the Camino Real Hotel in Mexico City, completed in 1968 to meet the demands of foreign visitors to the Olympics. Barragán was responsible for the landscaping, an important element of the design. Based around a large courtyard for social activities, with smaller patios lending privacy and seclusion to clusters of guest rooms, the lush enclave is refuge from the noise and distractions of the city.

From pre-Columbian days, Mexicans have lived in ample spaces with vibrant colours and varied textures. Perhaps the most significant characteristic of Mexican architecture and that which also identifies the work of Legorreta is the wall. The wall is part of the fabric of Mexico and Legorreta uses it as a building element and a symbol. Walls of pre-Columbian ceremonial centres not only defined spaces and enclosures but also added to the enigmatic quality and significance of sites. In Spain, walls were erected around a town as a means of defence, around a patio to circumscribe a living space and around churches to shape courtyards, creating places for religious celebration.

When the Hispanic and pre-Columbian cultures merged, the wall evolved to serve the special character of colonial Mexico. This type of Mexican wall can be found in the courtyards of sixteenth-century churches (built for both defensive and religious purposes), along village streets to separate the public from the private realm and in the local architecture that has evolved since colonial times. Walls can evoke notions of strength, power, struggle and peace. The wall is also a physical canvas for social and artistic expression, animated and elaborated by such great Mexican muralists as Diego Rivera (1886–1957), who exalted the indigenous and popular heritage in Mexican culture.

The tradition of the wall persists in the architecture of Ricardo Legorreta with the same spiritual intensity, but in a contemporary way. At the Renault factory in Durango (1985), he designed a long, low, terracotta-coloured wall that hovers behind the dunes, evoking the presence of the surrounding desert. Inside, the wall is more congenial: bright, sensuous and sheltering. Legorreta evocatively describes the complex as a fiesta of walls.

Legorreta's walls are usually sumptuously coloured, enriching and dramatizing space. Colour is the lifeblood of Mexico and Legorreta, like his distinguished mentor Luis Barragán, favours a vivid palette: taxi-cab yellow, ultramarine, violet, blood orange and magenta. Colour articulates openings in walls, breaks up the monolithic severity of large masses and creates a sense of depth. Sometimes it is used to generate visual mystery or surprise, at other times it is simply a source of delight. For example, at Managua's new Metropolitan Cathedral (1990–93, p 104) the austerity of raw concrete walls is softened by applied planes of shocking fuschia and yellow; for a major urban landscaping project at Pershing Square in Los Angeles (1991–94, p 108), a purple campanile soars over the city; and at a business park (Solana, Texas, 1991), blue barrel vaults enclose the entrance hall, reflecting and intensifying light as it permeates the space.

Changing light as a means of giving life to spaces is very important to Legorreta. Mexico's mountainous landscape, clear skies and hot climate generate a particular quality of natural light, exploited by Legorreta to orchestrate the effect of materials, planes and textures. Often his walls are perforated and screenlike, dramatically diffusing light into an interior while the presence of water produces magical, shimmering reflections.

Although Legorreta sets out to create a contemporary Mexican architecture, his work has an undeniable appeal beyond his native land. His first project outside Mexico was a house for Mexican actor Ricardo Montalbán high in the Hollywood hills (1985). The house presents a series of blank walls to the street to ensure privacy, again recalling traditional Mexican buildings, but beyond this enclosure the interior is light and open with stunning views over Los Angeles. More recently, Legorreta was selected to design the Mexican Museum of Art in San Francisco, principally for his ability to convey *mexicanidad* to an American audience concerned with an authentic sense of identity.

Having worked both in Mexico and abroad, Legorreta clearly sees his architecture as a means of asserting cultural independence. 'When I designed Automex it was like a strong yell. *"Viva México! Viva los Méxicanos! Viva yo!"* Why can't a country or a poor person have a right to be free? Why, simply because one is poor economically should one be restricted in talent, sensibility and dignity?'[2] Such energetic patriotism underscores Legorreta's commitment to his work and has enabled him to become one of the country's most successful architects, working for corporate clients and the state, with offices in Mexico City and Los Angeles. He has also taught at UCLA and the University of Austin in Texas, and is increasingly in demand for international lectures, juries and symposia.

At heart Legorreta remains besotted with his native country. The powerful forms of pre-Columbian architecture, the Hispanic baroque and the Mexican vernacular are all apparent in his work, filtered through a purifying screen of attention to composition, light and materials. Legorreta's descriptions of his own buildings are often rhapsodically poetic, reflecting the joy and exuberance of Mexico, but his architecture is also tempered and refined by wider, universal themes: rationalism and romance, mystery and logic, the importance of light, the pleasure of water, the tectonic quality of the wall, the vitality of colour. Though rooted in Mexico, Legorreta's work has a global resonance.

1 Wayne Attoe, ed., *The Architecture of Ricardo Legorreta* (Austin: The University of Texas Press, 1990), p 11

2 Ibid.

Metropolitan Cathedral
Managua, Nicaragua, 1990–93

In 1972, an earthquake devastated the Nicaraguan capital of Managua, destroying the city's Catholic cathedral. Restoration of the original Spanish Colonial building was considered impossible, so it was decided to establish a new cathedral on a different site. In a country traumatized by both natural disasters and violent political upheaval, this act assumed a profound spiritual and social significance. Nearly 90% of Nicaragua's population of 4 million is Catholic.

Ricardo Legorreta's design is a powerful response to the notion that liturgical space has changed from an awe-inspiring 'house of God', to a 'house of the community'. The towering side aisles are lined with pivoting oak doors and punctuated by fretted, timber screens painted virulent pink. Like the canary yellow selectively applied to the underside of the roof structure, and the flashes of carmine red on the external walls, the use of raw colour evokes a searing contrast with the rough, grey, in-situ concrete.

Attached to the main worshipping space are three smaller side chapels. A small baptistry is placed on the south-west corner and is illuminated by slits in the concrete walls and a single oculus overhead. Mass is celebrated every day in the Santisimo Chapel, a rectangular space with a cross-shaped aperture punched into one end of the wall. The scale and play of light creates an intimacy and calm appropriate to the daily Eucharistic celebration. There is a separate veneration chapel dedicated to the image of the 'Sangre de Christo', an ancient crucifix salvaged from Managua's original cathedral. From the outside the perforated silo of the chapel appears as a constelled dome of the heavens.

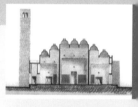

The roof structure is expressed as a dramatic cluster of onion domes, partly inspired by Kahn and partly by the Spanish presence in Nicaragua. The sixty-three domes admit light and ventilation, but their suggestively mammary appearance has, perhaps not surprisingly, disquieted some of the more conservative members of the congregation. Yet the building is popular and well used – open-air services in the esplanade in front of the cathedral can attract up to 100,000 celebrants.

Contemporary Art Museum
Monterrey, Mexico, 1988–91

2.42 Located on the city's Macroplaza, the museum is flanked by the cathedral and the seat of regional government. It exemplifies Legorreta's interest in the traditional hacienda form, where a central courtyard or patio is surrounded by arcades off which the rooms open. The hacienda model has often led Legorreta to create buildings with massive, almost imperforate walls, enclosing secret inner realms. Here the entrance is carved out of the main mass as a courtyard raised a few steps above street level. A huge abstract dove by Juan Soriano signals the entrance from afar and continues the twentieth-century Mexican tradition of closely allying contemporary art and architecture.

At the end of the entrance arcade, with its three fat blue columns, are the doors to the vestibule. This is a lofty hall which gives access to the auditorium, café, museum shop and central courtyard. The terracotta-coloured exterior is matched in the vestibule, suffusing the other white, internal walls with a reddish glow. A screen of sheet steel separates the vestibule from the central courtyard. The thin edges of the sheet form a square grid in delicate contrast to the plainness and solidity of the other walls. Looking through the screen the courtyard is revealed, but the vista is magically abstracted and dissected by the depth of the steel members.

The courtyard is a calm, space with arcades on three sides and the entire area is refreshed by the sound and presence of water in a shallow pool in the central part of the floor. Light is reflected off the pool, bathing the courtyard in a soft luminance. Galleries are arranged in enfilade around three sides of the courtyard. Generally top-lit, they offer a range of spaces and heights in which artwork can be displayed to the best advantage. Strategically placed windows and roof-lights keep the visitor in touch with the elements and the surrounding city.

Pershing Square
Los Angeles, California, 1991–94

Divided along the lines of income and race, downtown Los Angeles is virtually bereft of public urban space. Set aside by the city council in 1866 'for public use', the 5-acre (2-hectare) site – in effect a block of the street grid – has been radically redesigned by Ricardo Legorreta working with landscape architect Laurie Olin.

The block was too large to function as a single symmetrical space, so it was divided into two plazas linked by an east-west walkway. Inspired by sensuous Hispanic landscaping traditions of water and colour, the new square is a choreography of disparate elements unified by hard landscaping to create a series of lucid and complex spaces.

The focus of the composition is a soaring 125-foot-high (38.1 metre) cast-concrete campanile (in vivid purple), which serves as a vertical marker for the square, reminiscent of church towers in Mexico. At its base, water flows from an aqueduct into a large, circular pool, the focus of the southern plaza. Recalling the city's precarious geography, a stylized earthquake faultline (one of several commissioned works of art by Barbara McCarren) extends from the pavement to the pool. Two searing yellow buildings – a café and a triangular tourist centre – connect the south and north plazas.

In the northern plaza, boldly coloured walls punctured with geometric openings frame views and create gathering places. Sculptural, freestanding spheres and groves of palm trees identify and shape spaces, and lush bluegrass is used to soften the hard edges. Most of the square is paved in patterned, red-tinted concrete and crushed granite to reduce maintenance costs and to improve access for disabled people. With its bold forms and inventive landscaping, Pershing Square has been transformed into a civilized urban oasis, bringing much needed green space to downtown Los Angeles.

Office Building
Monterrey, Mexico, 1993–95

2.44 Completed in 1995, this office complex in Monterrey consists of two independent buildings, each with its own particular identity, yet both forming a coherent whole. One building is an office for a prominent businessman who also collects Mexican contemporary art, the other houses office space to let. Organization and massing were largely determined by the wedge-shaped site, while the modest scale addresses and responds to the suburban neighbourhood.

The main building takes the form of an eroded cube, with a central atrium providing orientation. At each level the atrium is rotated, allowing natural light to penetrate the interior. The main entrance hall contains artwork from the client's collection, so the space assumes the animated character of a small art gallery. The secondary office building is located on the prow of the site. Projected cubes cast shadows across the façade and provide protection from the harsh Mexican sunlight.

Walls and volumes create patios and terraces so that, in the archetypal Mediterranean tradition, external space becomes part of the complex. Terraces have views to the mountains, and the patios form sheltered and intimate courtyards. Strong colour is used to articulate the concrete wall planes: the main building combines a cadmium-yellow exterior with flashes of hot pink on the atrium walls; the speculative offices are rendered a more muted terracotta. The use of such intense colours allied to a morphology of broad horizontal volumes punctuated by sculptural elements energetically synthesizes and reinterprets the architectural spirit of pre-Columbian, colonial and vernacular Mexico. Even for such a comparatively prosaic brief, the outcome is a startling yet seductive architectural language, rooted in context and culture. It demonstrates Legorreta's continuing interest in traditional Mexican typologies and spatial devices without descending into kitsch or pseudo-vernacular.

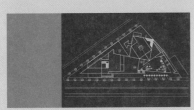

2.41 Metropolitan Cathedral
The new cathedral is by far the largest building to be built in Managua for at least a decade. Its sheer scale and haunting beauty makes it stand out from its surroundings yet still be part of them. The scrawny finger of the campanile presides over a cluster of mammarian domes.

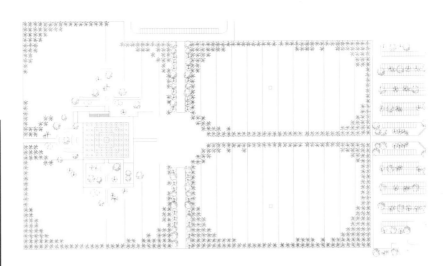

2.41 Metropolitan Cathedral
Planes of scintillating colour animate the rough concrete walls, breaking up the monumental scale. Light filters down from domed rooflights into the cavernous main nave, which has a capacity for 1,000 worshippers. The floor is inlaid with a geometric pattern of handmade concrete tiles.

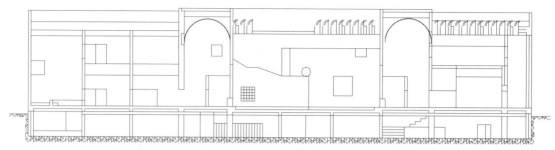

2.42 Contemporary Art Museum
The giant dove marks the museum's
entrance court, which in turn
anchors the building to Monterrey's
central plaza. Hermetic, terracotta-
coloured walls enclose the
museum, but inside, light and
water trickle through the cool,
luminous spaces. The pool-filled
central courtyard also acts as a
reception space.

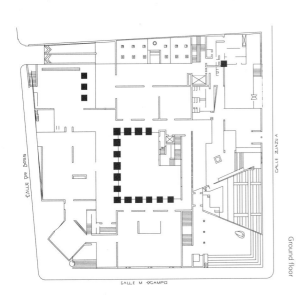

Ground floor

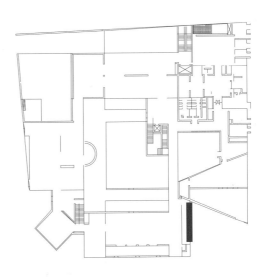

Second floor

2.43 Pershing Square
Opening up the urban landscape, the public square is the size of a city block. Boldly scaled and coloured elements combine with hard and soft landscaping to form a refuge from the blare and bustle of Los Angeles.

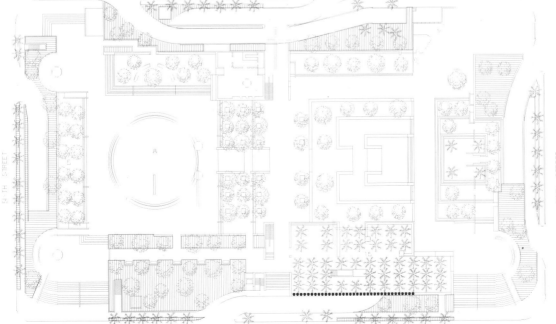

OLIVE STREET

5TH STREET

HILL STREET

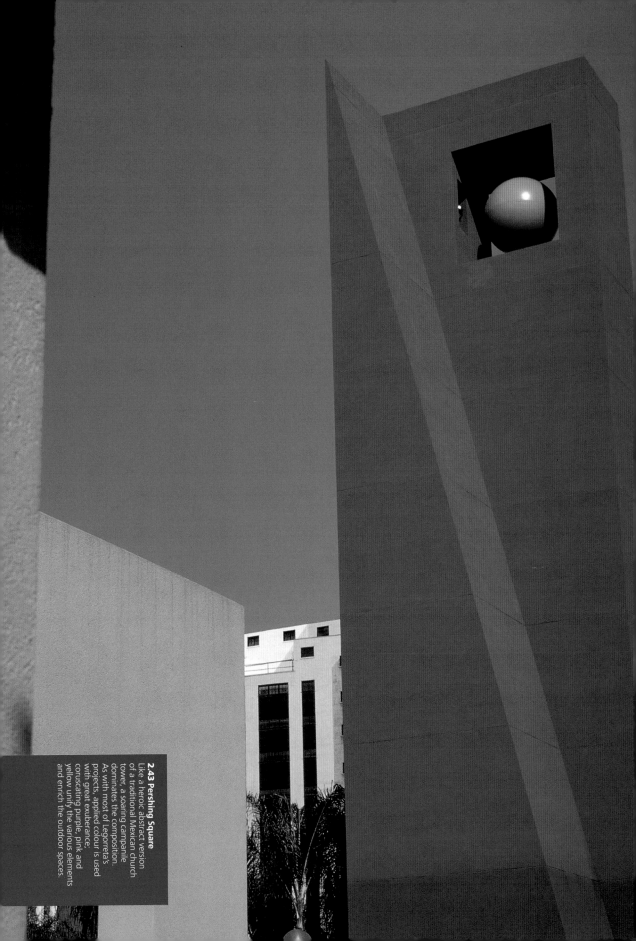

2.43 Pershing Square
Like a heroic abstract version of a traditional Mexican church tower, a soaring campanile dominates the composition. As with most of Legorreta's projects, applied colour is used with great exuberance; coruscating purple, pink and yellow unify the various elements and enrich the outdoor spaces.

2.44 Office Building
The building consists of a small lettable office block and a larger headquarters for a prominent businessman and his art collection. The stepped, terraced forms recall the mountain landscape, and strong colour energizes the surroundings.

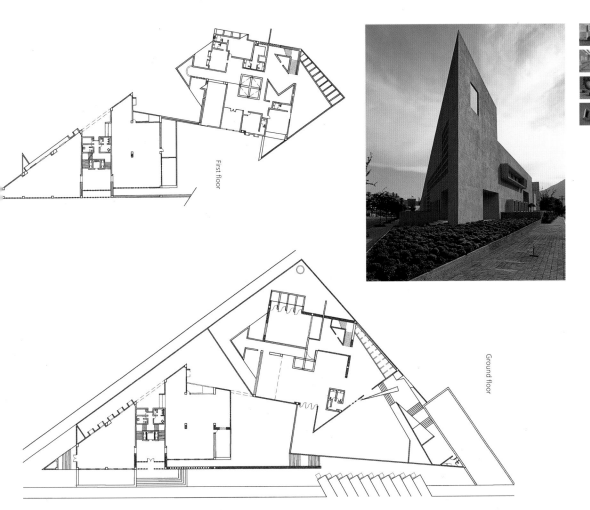

First floor

Ground floor

2.44 Office Building
In Hispanic tradition, walls and volumes are inventively used to form patios and outdoor spaces that provide shade and extend the inner realm. Intimate courtyards are enclosed by blind walls and planting softens the austere geometry and adds organic luxuriance to the organic luxuriance to the network of spaces. The modest scale responds to the suburban context.

Antoine Predock

Biographical notes

Born in Lebanon, Missouri in 1936, Antoine Predock studied engineering and architecture at the University of New Mexico, Albuquerque from 1957 to 1961. He then spent the following year at Columbia University, New York and has been in private practice in Albuquerque since 1967. Through a succession of challenging projects that draw deeply on nuances of site and context, Predock has made the transition from American Southwest regionalist to an architect of national and international stature.

Select bibliography

Monographs

Antoine Predock Architect 2, Brad Collins and Elizabeth Zimmermann (eds) (New York: Rizzoli, 1998)

Turtle Creek House, Antoine Predock (New York: The Monacelli Press, 1998)

'Antoine Predock', *Korean Architect* (special monograph issue, no 152, April 1997)

Antoine Predock, Geoffrey Baker (Architectural Monograph, no 49, London: Academy Editions, 1997)

Architectural Journeys, Antoine Predock (New York: Rizzoli, 1995)

Antoine Predock Architect, Brad Collins and Juliette Robbins (eds) (New York: Rizzoli, 1994)

'Antoine Predock', *A + U* (special monograph issue, vol 218, November 1988)

Articles/Features

'Arizona Science Centre, Phoenix', *Architecture* (vol 86, no 7, July 1997): 94–101

'Arizona Science Centre, Phoenix', *GA Document* (no 53, 1997): 20–29

Architecture after Modernism, Diane Ghirardo (London: Thames & Hudson, 1996): 59–61, 79–82, 141–43

Contemporary American Architects: Volume II, Philip Jodidio, (Cologne: Taschen Verlag, 1996): 128–41

'Desert Education', *Architecture* (March 1995)

'New buildings by Antoine Predock', *Architecture* (vol 83, no 3, March 1995)

'Turtle Creek House, Dallas', *GA Houses* (no 42, June 1994): 78–93

'Turtle Creek House, Dallas', *Architectural Record* (vol 182, no 4, April 1994): 76–83

'Border Crossings', *Architecture* (vol 80, no 8, August 1991): 58–63

'Nelson Fine Arts Centre, Tempe', *L'Arca* (no 47, March 1991): 10–21

'Nelson Fine Arts Centre, Tempe', *Arquitectura Viva* (no 15, November/December 1990): 24–28

'Interview with Antoine Predock', *Architecture Intérieure CREE* (no 233, December/January 1989–90): 104–5

'Nelson Fine Arts Centre, Tempe', *GA Document* (no 24, August 1989): 6–19

'Nelson Fine Arts Centre, Tempe', *Progressive Architecture* (vol 70, June 1989): 65–77

'Rio Grande Nature Centre', *Spazio e Società* (vol 12, no 46, April/June 1989): 122–33

'Out of Albuquerque', *Architectural Record* (vol 176, no 12, October 1988): 88–97

'Meet the Architect – Antoine Predock', *GA Houses* (no 21, February 1987): 74–115

'Reinterpreting Regionalism: New Mexico', *Architecture* (vol 73, no 13, March 1984): 120–28

Project information

Nelson Fine Arts Center 1985–89

Project team Jon Anderson, Geoffrey Beebe, John Fleming, Ronald Jacob, Antoine Predock, Tim Rohleder, Kevin Spence

General contractor Westbrook

Structural engineer Robin E Park Associates

Services engineer Baltes Valentino

Landscape consultant James Abell

Photography Timothy Hursley

Turtle Creek House 1987–93

Project team Geoffrey Beebe, John Brittingham, Jorg Burbano, Paul Gonzales, David Nelson, Antoine Predock

Structural engineer James F Smith

Services engineer MEP Systems

Landscape consultant Rosa Finsley

Photography Timothy Hursley

Arizona Science Center 1990–97

Project team Geoffrey Beebe, John Brittingham, Linda Christensen, Mark Donahue, Nancy Napheys, George Newlands, Antoine Predock

Associate architect Cornoyer-Hendrick

General contractor SundtCorp

Structural engineer Robin E Park Associates

Services engineer Baltes Valentino

Acoustic consultant McKay Conant Brook

Theatre consultant IWERKS

Photography Timothy Hursley

Rio Grande Nature Center 1978–82

Project team Geoffrey Beebe, Ronald Jacob, Antoine Predock

General contractor John R Lavis

Structural engineer Randy Holt and Associates

Services engineer Coupland Powell Morgan Associates

Photography Timothy Hursley

Tadao Ando

Biographical notes

Tadao Ando is a self-taught architect. He was born in Osaka, Japan in 1941 and as a young man travelled to the United States, Europe and Africa. He established his own practice in 1969 in Osaka and has since realized a considerable body of work in Japan and a handful of overseas projects. Using unadorned materials and simple forms, Ando captures an austere elementalism that has its roots in traditional Japanese art and architecture. He has taught at various American universities, including Yale, Columbia and Harvard and his work has been widely exhibited.

Select bibliography

Monographs

Ando Architect, Kazukiyo Matsuba (Tokyo: Kodansha International, 1998)

Tadao Ando Architecture and Spirit, Anatxu Zabalbeasco and Javier Rodriguez Marcos (eds) (Barcelona: Editorial Gustavo Gili, 1998)

Church on the Water/Church of Light, Philip Drew (London: Phaidon Press, 1996)

Tadao Ando, Masao Furuyama (Basel: Birkhäuser, 1996)

Tadao Ando: The Colours of Light, Richard Pare (London: Phaidon Press, 1996)

'Tadao Ando', *GA Document Extra* (special monograph issue, no 1, 1995)

Tadao Ando Complete Works, Francesco Dal Co (ed) (London: Phaidon Press, 1995)

Tadao Ando: vol 2 Yukio Futagawa (ed), criticism Tom Heneghan (Tokyo: A. D. A. Edita, 1993)

'Tadao Ando', *Japan Architect* (special monograph issue, no 1, January 1991)

Tadao Ando: vol 1 Yukio Futagawa (ed), criticism Kenneth Frampton (Tokyo: A. D. A. Edita, 1987)

Articles/Features

'Ando's Couture Concrete: Restrained Yet Revolutionary', *Concrete Quarterly* (no 191, Summer 1999): 6–8

'Bauen mit Beton' ('Building with Concrete'), *Detail* (vol 37, no 8, December 1997):1326–29

'Tadao Ando's Royal Gold Medal Address' *Concrete Quarterly* (no 184, Autumn 1997): 2–7

'Church of Light, Ibaraki', *Arquitectura* (Madrid, no 311, 1997): 75–77

'Meditation space, UNESCO, Paris', *The Architectural Review* (vol 199, no 1190, April 1996): 20–21

'Meditation space, UNESCO, Paris', *Deutsche Bauzeitschrift* (vol 44, no 4, April 1996): 34–35

Theorizing a New Agenda for Architecture: An Anthology of Architectural Theory 1965–1995, Kate Nesbitt (ed) (New York: Princeton Architectural Press, 1996)

'Realms of the Living and Dead, Chikatsu-Asuka Historical Museum', *Architectural Record* (vol 183, no 11, November 1995): 72–77

'Chikatsu-Asuka Historical Museum', *The Architectural Review* (vol 198, no 1182, August 1995): 40–44

'Tatami Matting and Flying Walls', *Architekt* (no 8, August 1995): 471–75

'Chikatsu-Asuka Historical Museum', *Casabella* (vol 59, no 622, April 1995): 52–57

'Concrete Poetics: Reconsidering Tadao Ando', *ANY* (Architecture New York, no 6, May/June 1994): 7–47

Contemporary Japanese Architects, Dirk Meyhofer (Cologne: Taschen Verlag, 1994)

'Conversation avec Ando', *Architecture d'Aujourd'hui* (no 286, April 1993)

'Hompukuji Water Temple, Awaji', *Domus* (no 742, October 1992): 29–37

'Hompukuji Water Temple, Awaji', *GA Document* (no 35, 1992): 60–69

'Ando le poète du béton' ('Ando the Concrete Poet'), *D'Architectures* (no 15, May 1991)

'Architetture sacrali di Tadao Ando' ('Tadao Ando's Sacred Buildings'), *Casabella* (vol 53, no 558, June 1989)

'Church of Light, Ibaraki', *Japan Architect* (no 6, June 1989): 6–19

'Church of Light, Ibaraki', *GA Document* (no 22, January 1989): 88–89

'Japan', *The Architectural Review* (special issue, vol 182, no 1089, November 1987)

Project information

Church of the Light 1987–89

General contractor   Tatsumi Construction

Structural engineer   Ascoral Engineering Associates

Photography   Tadao Ando, Mitsuo Matsuoka/ *Japan Architect*

Chikatsu-Asuka Historical Museum 1990–94

General contractors   Konolke Construction, Mitsubishi Construction

Structural engineer   Ascoral Engineering Associates

Services engineer   Setubi Giken

Photography   Mitsuo Matsuoka/*Japan Architect*, Shigeo Ogawa/*Japan Architect*

Meditation Space, UNESCO 1994–95

Photography   Tadao Ando, Stéphane Couturier/*Archipress*

Hompukuji Water Temple 1989–91

Photography   Tadao Ando, Hiroshi Ueda/ *Japan Architect*

Wiel Arets

Biographical notes

Wiel Arets was born in 1955 in Heerlen, The Netherlands. He studied architecture at the Technical University of Eindhoven and graduated in 1983. In 1984, Arets set up his own practice in Heerlen and between 1985 and 1989 he travelled extensively in Russia, Japan, America and Europe. He taught at London's Architectural Association from 1988 to 1992. Characterized by a stark clarity and economy, his work is informed by diverse sources and reflects his extensive writings, yet it also leaves space for individual interpretation and imagination.

Select bibliography

Monographs

Wiel Arets, Manfred Bock (Rotterdam: 010 Publishers, 1998)

El Croquis (special monograph issue, no 85, 1997)

Wiel Arets, Bart Lootsma (ed) (exhibition catalogue, Antwerp: International Kunstcentrum de Singe, 1996)

'Wiel Arets', *A + U* (special monograph issue, no 281, February, 1994)

An Alabaster Skin, Wiel Arets (Rotterdam: 010 Publishers, 1992)

Wiel Arets Architect (Rotterdam: 010 Publishers, 1989)

Articles/Features

'The Dutch Model in Architecture, Urban Design and Landscape Design', Wiel Arets, *SD* (special issue, no 413, February 1999): 57–60

'From Amsterdam to Rotterdam', *A+V Monografia* (special issue, no 73, September/October 1998): 44–53

'Police Station, Vaals', *Baumeister* (vol 95, no 3, March 1998): 18–25

'AZL Pension Fund Headquarters, Heerlen', *UME* (no 8, 1998): 54–65

'Police Station, Vaals', *Archithèse* (vol 27, no 3, May/June 1997): 30–33

'Image and Land: Strategies for Dynamic Contextualism', *De Architect* (vol 28, no 3, March 1997): 58–69

'Police Station, Vaals', *Deutsche Bauzeitschrift* (vol 44, no 12, December 1996): 32–33

'AZL Pension Fund Headquarters, Heerlen', *The Architectural Review* (vol 199, no 1190, April 1996): 50–53

'Conjugal Cunning: Recent Work by Wiel Arets', *Archis* (no 4, April 1996): 18–29

'Police Station, Vaals', *Domus* (no 781, April 1996): 30–34

'AZL Pension Fund Headquarters, Heerlen', *GA Document* (no 48, 1996): 46–55

'Police Station, Vaals', *Arkitekten* (vol 98, no 11, 1996): 28–30

'Dialogue in the Work of Wiel Arets', *De Architect* (vol 26, November 1995): 46–75

'Housing in Tilburg', *Casabella* (vol 59, no 628, November 1995): 54–63

'Maastricht Academy of Arts', *The Architectural Review* (vol 198, no 1183, September 1995): 48–52

'Maastricht Academy of Arts', *Progressive Architecture* (vol 76, June 1995): 102–3

'Maastricht Academy of Arts', *Arquitectura Viva* (no 38, September/October 1994): 62–67

'Maastricht Academy of Arts', *Blueprint* (no 110, September 1994): 42–43

'Maastricht Academy of Arts', *Domus* (no 757, February 1994): 23–29

'Maastricht Academy of Arts', *Archis* (November 1993): 17–27

'Continuing Dialogue: Translucent Architecture', *Skala* (no 28, 1993): 56–63

'Recent Work of Wiel Arets and Wim van der Bergh', *AA Files* (no 21, Spring 1991): 16–25

Project information

Academy of Arts Extension 1989–93

Project team	Wiel Arets, René Holten, Jo Janssen, Anita Morandini, Maurice Paulussen
General contractor	Laudy Bouw & Planontwikkeling
Structural engineer	Grabowsky & Poort
Services engineer	Coman Raadgevende
Cost consultant	Bremen Bouwadviseurs
Photography	Kim Zwarts

Apartment Blocks 1992–94

Project team	Wiel Arets, Reina Bos, Tina Brandt, Paulus Egers, Michel Melenhorst, Andrea Wallrath
Photography	Kim Zwarts

Regional Police Headquarters 1993–95

Project team	Wiel Arets, Eric Bolle, Delphine Clavien, Rhea Harbers, René Holten, Michel Melenhorst
Structural engineer	A Palte
Photography	Kim Zwarts

AZL Pension Fund Headquarters 1990–95

Project team	Wiel Arets, Jo Janssen, Dominic Papa, Maurice Paulussen, René Thijssen, Hein Urlings, Ani Velez, Richard Welten
Structural engineer	Grabowsky & Poort
Services engineer	Tema
Cost consultant	Bremen Bouwadviseurs
Photography	Kim Zwarts

Ricardo Legorreta

Biographical notes

Born in Mexico City in 1931, Ricardo Legorreta studied at the Universidad Nacional Autónoma de Mexico from 1948 to 1952. Legorreta then spent two years working for José Villagran García in Mexico City and subsequently became his partner in 1955. Five years later, Legorreta established his own practice. His work has evolved out of the study and understanding of the values of traditional architecture in Mexico fused with the social ideals of modernism. Along with Luis Barragán, he is one of Mexico's most distinguished contemporary architects.

Select bibliography

Monographs

Ricardo Legorreta, John V Mutlow (London: Thames & Hudson, 1997)

'Ricardo Legorreta', *A + U* (special monograph issue, no 265, October 1992)

The Architecture of Ricardo Legorreta, Wayne Attoe (ed) (Austin: The University of Texas Press, 1990)

Articles/Features

'Balanced Madness', *World Architecture* (no 68, July/August 1998): 62–63

'Interview with Ricardo Legorreta', *Architecture of Israel* (no 34, Summer 1998): 87–91

'Country Focus – Mexico', *World Architecture* (no 53, February 1997)

Arquitectos Mexicanos: Entre La Tradicion y La Modernidad, Fernando de Haro Lebrija and Omar Fuentes Elizondo (eds) (Mexico City: Attame Ediciones, 1997)

'Managua Cathedral', *Arquitectura* (Madrid, no 311, 1997): 59–65

Modernity and the Architecture of Mexico, Edward R Burian (Austin: The University of Texas Press, 1997)

'Ricardo Legorreta', *Arquitectura* (Mexico City, no 15, January/February 1996)

Mexico 90s Una Arquitectura Contemporánea, Miguel Adrià (Barcelona: Editorial Gustavo Gili, 1996)

'Latin America', *L'Arca* (special issue, no 93, May 1995)

'Legorreta e il populismo' ('Legorreta and Populism'), *Casabella* (vol 59, no 621, March 1995): 40–41

'Mexico', *Arquitectura Viva* (special issue, no 40, January/February 1995)

The Architecture of Latin America, Miguel Roca (ed) (London: Academy Editions, 1995)

'Pershing Square', *Progressive Architecture* (vol 75, no 1, September 1994): 45–46

'Pershing Square', *The Architectural Review* (vol 196, no 1169, July 1994): 68–73

'Managua Cathedral', *Projeto* (no 173, April 1994): 60–61

'Pershing Square', *Architecture* (vol 83, no 4, April 1994): 21

'Colour Confessions by Contemporary Architects', *Daidalos* (no 51, March 1994): 24–43

'Fond Memories of Place: Luis Barragán and Ricardo Legorreta', *Places* (vol 9, no 1, Winter 1994): 34–43

'Regionalism and the Vanguard', *World Architecture* (no 21, January 1993): 48–51

'Interview with Ricardo Legorreta', *MIMAR* (no 43, June 1992): 62–67

'Ricardo Legorreta y la arquitectura mexicana', *Projecto* (no 150, March 1992): 30–43

'Contemporary Art Museum, Monterrey', *The Architectural Review* (vol 190, no 1139, January 1992)

'South of the Border', *Blueprint* (no 66, April 1990): 56–57

'Contemporary Art Museum, Monterrey', *Arquitectura Viva* (no 8, October 1989)

Seis Arquitectos Mexicanos, Jorge Glusberg (Buenos Aires: Ediciones de Arte Gaglionne, 1983)

Project information

Metropolitan Cathedral 1990–93

Project team	Miguel Almaraz, Noé Castro, Ricardo Legorreta, Víctor Legorreta, Guillermo Díaz de Sandi, Francisco Vivas
Structural engineer	Walker P Moore
Services engineer	Lamsa Ingenieros
Photography	Lourdes Legorreta

Contemporary Art Museum 1988–91

Project team	Noé Castro, Erica Krayer, Ricardo Legorreta, Víctor Legorreta, Joaquin Pineda, Carlos Villela
General contractor	Rafael Garza
Structural engineer	Raúl Izquierdo
Services engineer	Calefacción y Ventilación
Photography	Lourdes Legorreta

Pershing Square 1991–94

Project team	Geraldo Alonso, Noé Castro, Ricardo Legorreta, Víctor Legorreta
Associate architect	Langdon Wilson
Structural engineer	Nabith Yussef & Associates
Artist	Barbara McCarren
Photography	Lourdes Legorreta

Office Building 1993–95

Project team	Miguel Almaraz, Noé Castro, Héctor Cavazos, Ricardo Legorreta, Víctor Legorreta
General contractors	Centro de Construcción, Lauro Chapa
Structural engineers	DYS, Alejandro Fierro
Services engineers	Hecnie y Asociados, Héctor Nieto, Alejandro Borboa
Photography	Lourdes Legorreta

Illustration credits
(pp 1–23) **Frontmatter**: p 1 Nelson Fine Arts Center (Antoine Predock); p 2 Turtle Creek House (Antoine Predock); p 3 Church of the Light (Tadao Ando); p 4 Hompukuji Water Temple (Tadao Ando); p 5 AZL Pension Fund Headquarters (Wiel Arets); p 6 AZL Pension Fund Headquarters (Wiel Arets); p 7 Contemporary Art Museum (Ricardo Legorreta); p 8 Office Building (Ricardo Legorreta); pp 10–11 Chikatsu-Asuka Historical Museum (Wiel Arets); **Introduction**: p 14 Natalie Tepper/Arcaid; p 16 Julius Shulman/The Architectural Press; p 17 *Guernica*, 1937 by Pablo Picasso (1881–1973), Museo Centro de Arte Reina Sofia, Madrid, Spain/Bridgeman Art Library; p 18 G E Kidder-Smith/The Architectural Press; p 19 Ezra Stoller/Esto/Arcaid; p 20 Ezra Stoller/ Esto/The Architectural Press; p 21 Nicolau Drei/The Architectural Press; p 22 Gabriele Basilico/The Architectural Press; p 23 Lourdes Legorreta

Cover design: *background image* Arizona Science Center (Antoine Predock, photograph by Timothy Hursley); *front, from left* Nelson Fine Arts Center (photograph by Timothy Hursley), Chikatsu-Asuka Historical Museum (photograph by *Japan Architect*), Regional Police Headquarters (photograph by Kim Zwarts), Office Building (photograph by Lourdes Legorreta); *back, from left* Arizona Science Center (photograph by Timothy Hursley), Meditation Space (photograph by Stéphane Couturier/*Archipress*), Apartment Blocks (photograph by Kim Zwarts), Pershing Square (photograph by Lourdes Legorreta); *back flap, from top* Arizona Science Center (photograph by Timothy Hursley), Meditation Space (photograph by Tadao Ando), Regional Police Headquarters (photograph by Kim Zwarts), Office Building (photograph by Lourdes Legorreta); *inside cover, front* Nelson Fine Arts Center (Antoine Predock, photograph by Timothy Hursley); *inside cover, back* Academy of Arts (Wiel Arets, photograph by Kim Zwarts)

© 2000 Thames & Hudson Ltd, London

First published in paperback in the United States of America in 2000 by Thames & Hudson Inc., 500 Fifth Avenue, New York, New York 10110

Library of Congress Catalog Card Number 00-101068
ISBN 0-500-28227-7

Printed and bound in China by Everbest Printing Co. Ltd.